Hal Betancourt

THE ADVERTISING ANSWERBOOK

A Guide for Business and Professional People

A SPECTRUM BOOK

PRENTICE-HALL, INC., Englewood Cliffs, New Jersey 07632

Library of Congress Cataloging in Publication Data

Betancourt, Hal.
  The advertising answerbook.

  "A Spectrum Book."
  Includes index.
  1. Advertising—Handbooks, manuals, etc.
I. Title.
HF5823.B47   659.1'02'02   81-17757
                                 AACR2

ISBN 0-13-014514-9

ISBN 0-13-014506-8 {PBK.}

To my mother
Concepcion Jimenez Betancourt
who, when there was no money,
found enough to start me
on my career

10 9 8 7 6 5 4 3 2 1

A SPECTRUM BOOK. Printed in the United States of America.

Editorial production/supervision
   and interior design by *Heath Lynn Silberfeld*
Manufacturing buyer: *Barbara A. Frick*
Art direction by *Jeannette Jacobs*
Cover illustration by *Bob Aiese*

This Spectrum Book is available to businesses and organizations
at a special discount when ordered in large quantities. For
information, contact Prentice-Hall, Inc., General Book Publishing Division,
Special Sales, Englewood Cliffs, N.J. 07632.

Prentice-Hall International, Inc., *London*
Prentice-Hall of Australia Pty. Limited, *Sydney*
Prentice-Hall of Canada, Ltd., *Toronto*
Prentice-Hall of India Private Limited, *New Delhi*
Prentice-Hall of Japan, Inc., *Tokyo*
Prentice-Hall of Southeast Asia Pte. Ltd., *Singapore*
Whitehall Books Limited, *Wellington, New Zealand*

CONTENTS

FOREWORD

In his unforgettable book about the rabbits of *Watership Down*, Richard Adams describes an affliction that the rabbits call "Tharn." "Tharn" occurs when a rabbit who is crossing a road at night is suddenly caught in the glare of the headlights of an oncoming car and held transfixed there until tragedy strikes. Adams might well have been referring to a widespread affliction of business owners and managers when they are caught in the glitter and clatter of the advertising industry.

When faced with choices between TV, radio, newspaper, magazine, outdoor, specialties, and their endless varieties, the business-person may be a captive of "tharn" and do nothing until tragedy overtakes the business.

The Advertising Answerbook dispels the indecision of advertising "tharn" and gets us back to work planning budgets; selecting media; managing artists, photographers, and all the other professionals who make up the advertising industry. If the budget is limited, we find we can even write the copy and paste up the artwork.

The Advertising Answerbook shows us the way to cope with elusive problems by providing concrete step-by-step procedures and illustrations that help to blow away the fog of vague terminology. Once again, the businessperson can feel tht he or she has advertising under control.

Business venturing is not for those who wish to apply a proven formula to an identical problem each day and collect their fee. Businesspeople must constantly cope with uncertainty, and the advertising program may well be the most "ad-venturous" part of the enterprise.

John Lyman
Marketing Consultant
San Diego, California

PREFACE

When I first began teaching advertising classes through the San Diego Community Colleges Adult Education Program, I looked for a book to use as a text for my students. These were adults, new to advertising, who were in need of information they could apply in their businesses. I searched the local book stores, libraries, and university book shops. I found many well-written books on advertising, but most were too technical in content, didn't offer enough substance, were written for the large-budget national advertiser, or dealt with only one facet of advertising.

I decided to write the material myself, gearing it to the needs of the person who was inexperienced in the advertising field. It took the form of a weekly column, entitled "Advertising Basics," which, in addition to using as a text for my classes, I syndicated to several newspapers and magazines.

Each column reviewed a specific advertising subject in terms that could be understood by a non-advertising person. I crammed the columns with as much practical information and as many usable ideas as I could gather.

Many of the columns were sent to practicing professionals for their advice and comments on the validity and accuracy of the information. They responded with helpful suggestions that were also incorporated.

This book is a compilation of those columns. Some remain unchanged, a few are revised, and a great deal of the material is completely new.

From the beginning, the material in the book has been designed for and will be of most value to the following: (1) individuals who own their own businesses and must make sound advertising decisions that can affect the success or failure of their enterprises; (2) advertising managers and marketing directors, responsible for their company's advertising efforts, who must generate sales that will eventually be reflected in increased profits; (3) on-the-job advertising trainees who find themselves on the firing line with little or no time for additional training; (4) students who want to prepare themselves for careers in this wonderful, crazy business we call advertising.

The pages are filled with data on the mechanics, functions, and practices of advertising. Practical tips and helpful suggestions are liberally sprinkled throughout the book. For clarity's sake, advertising trade terms and buzz words have been kept to a minimum. A glossary is provided to define the most commonly used trade terms.

You will find useful information on the following: guidelines for establishing an advertising budget; how to measure advertising space and calculate rates; how to figure cost per thousand (CPM) to get the most value for your advertising dollar; an easy-to-remember formula for writing an ad; what you shouldn't say in your advertising message; how to get those walking fingers to stop at your yellow pages ad; how to work with commercial artists and photographers; a simple explanation of the different printing methods; and much, much more.

In addition, I have tried to anticipate those questions that are frequently asked about the advertising business—questions such as "How much should be set aside for an advertising budget?" "What are some things you can do for yourself when it comes to advertising?" "How can you avoid costly waste and stretch your advertising dollar?" "What services do agencies provide, and how much do they charge?" "What is the 15 percent agency commission, and who pays it?"

If you don't know the answers to questions such as these, you will by the time you finish this book. The answers are all here.

The book can serve as both a working tool and a reference source. Read it and use all the information you can, now. Keep it handy; refer to it every time the need arises.

Remember, if you are to be successful in advertising, you must have an understanding of what you are doing—no matter who you are or how much you are investing. I hope that this book will further that understanding.

Good luck!

Hal Betancourt

acknowledgments

For their assistance and encouragement in the preparation of this book, I am forever grateful to the following:

Aliton M. Fairchild, who introduced me to the world of writing and inspired me to teach, making this book possible.

Janet Lockman Caulk, for her invaluable advice, suggestions, and efforts in preparing the material contained in these pages.

My wife Lucia, for her faith and help in those early years that brought me to this point.

credits

A special thanks to the following for their assistance and permission to reprint certain portions of the material: Dick Tullar and Gerry Wilson, San Diego Union/Tribune; Lee Kerry, Editor, ADWEEK/West; Newspaper Advertising Bureau; Susan Spohn and F. Bradley Lynch, N. W. Ayer—ABH International; Harry Volk, Jr., Volk Corporation; Edward R. Des-Roches, Publisher, Heritage/Himmah Publications; H. W. Seidl, Jr. and Bob Townsend, Foster & Kleiser; Judy Meeker, Pacific Telephone; Pat Preuss, San Diego Gas & Electric Company.

about the author

Hal Betancourt, an advertising agency principal, has been awarded the Certificate of Merit from the Art Directors Club of New York and a Citation of Excellence from the First Advertising Agency Network. He currently writes the "Advertising Basics" column in business publications and conducts national advertising workshops and seminars.

ADVERTISING AGENCIES

what an agency does

"Advertising agencies are independent firms composed of creative and business people who develop, prepare and place advertising in advertising media for sellers seeking to find customers for their goods and services," says Maurice Mandell in *Advertising*. And if you are a business owner, you probably realize you must do some form of advertising to create sales and attract customers for your business. An advertising agency can be very helpful in your efforts. But you may have only a vague idea of what advertising agencies can do for you. How do they function? How do they charge for their services? How do you find one that best fits your needs?

Stay with me for a few minutes and I'll try to guide you through the advertising agency maze.

There are thousands of ad agencies, large and small, scattered across the country, from Madison Avenue to San Diego. Although they range in size from small one-person shops to the giant departmentalized advertising agencies employing hundreds of people, and with billings in the millions of dollars, their fundamental purposes are the same, to do the following: (1) plan the client's total advertising program; (2) select and contract for the media in which the advertising will appear; (3) prepare the advertising message (copy, layout, artwork, photography, etc.); (4) produce the finished advertising in the form required by the different media; (5) handle all record keeping and accounting for the client—to verify that the ad appears as requested and, upon receiving payment from the client, to pay the media's bills promptly.

Let's put that on instant replay and run it through again, slower. The agency does the following:

1. Plans the client's advertising program. It begins by becoming familiar with the client's company—its products and services. The agency studies various approaches to increase the client's sales based on market surveys, research reports, and their own past experiences. After the approach has been established, it is recommended to the client for approval.

2. With the client's approval, the agency then selects and contracts for the media (newspapers, magazines, radio, television, etc.) in which the advertising will appear. The agency's media department analyzes potential media to determine which are best suited to deliver the client's message most effectively, and at the lowest cost per advertising dollar. The agency then works up a media schedule (usually for a 12-month period) and submits it to the client for approval or revision.

3. Once the media schedule has been finalized and approved,

the agency prepares the advertising. Creating the advertising is the responsibility of a talented team of professionals. With market studies and research reports guiding them, and with a thorough knowledge of the client's product, this creative team arrives at a sales approach. Words are written, illustrations are suggested, and layouts (or TV storyboards) are designed. Once again, the client must approve the work performed on his or her behalf.

4. After the copy and layouts are approved, the agency produces the finished advertising in the form required by the different media. Each medium has its own requirements for the type of material it needs for reproduction. A newspaper printed by letterpress may require engravings, a magazine published by offset lithography will need litho negatives, a radio station will ask for taped commercials, and a television station wants either videotape or film. Generally speaking, the physical production of the advertising is not done by the agency. Instead, the work is done by outside sources, such as illustrators, art studios, photographers, typesetters, engravers, printers, film production houses, recording studios, and the like. The finished ads are approved by the client and sent to the various media before their closing dates (deadlines).

5. The agency then handles all record keeping and accounting for the client. Upon publication or broadcast, each medium sends the agency an invoice and proof of performance (with magazines and newspapers, it is in the form of tearsheets; and with the broadcast media, a notarized affidavit is submitted). The agency examines the invoices to verify that the advertising ran as ordered and that all bills from suppliers are fair and accurate. An itemized invoice is prepared to cover all costs incurred in producing the ad and is sent to the client for payment. When the client pays the agency, the agency then pays the individual suppliers.

the different types of ad agencies

There are three basic forms of advertising agencies: the full-service agency, the à la carte agency, and the in-house agency.

Briefly, they differ in the following ways:

Full-Service Agencies: Full-service agencies normally have a large staff and offer a wide range of services, as the name implies. Much of the work is done internally; the overflow is jobbed out to independent suppliers. Their fee is usually based on a minimum monthly retainer with some or all of the media commissions being retained by the agency. Creative services are charged on an hourly basis, and the rates will vary depending on the talent required. All outside supplier costs are billed to the client at net, plus a service charge. Full-service agencies are geared to handle the work of advertisers with an annual minimum ad budget of $50,000 or more. If you have a modest budget, you might end up feeling like a small fish in a big pond with a full-service agency.

A la carte Agencies: A la carte agencies are typically small, one- or two-person shops. Most of the creative work is done by free-lance talent for the à la carte agency. Many of these agencies are professional, but unfortunately not all of them are. Some of the owners are limited in knowledge to their own area of experience. This expertise is usually in one medium, and they are rank amateurs when it comes to areas with which they are not familiar. In truth, some are learning the business at the client's expense. A la carte agencies usually work on a project basis; no monthly retainer is required. If you need only one ad or brochure, they can handle it profitably since they don't have the high overhead of a full-service agency. This type of small shop normally requires the client to pay part of the cost in advance, with the balance due on completion. When negotiating with an à la carte agency, make sure you have a firm understanding as to what the total cost of the project will include *before* the work is begun. Ask whether it will include artwork, typography, photography, printing, and so on.

In-house Agencies: In-house agencies are a do-it-yourself form of advertising agency. Any company with the price of a business license can start its own in-house agency. There is no special training, credential, or proof of financial responsibility required. Any business-person can form an in-house agency, then proceed to buy creative work outside, place the advertising, and retain the 15% commission allowed by some of the local media (national media do not, as a rule, recognize this type of agency). In effect, the company goes into the advertising business. Among those who can logically justify setting up an in-house agency are large retailers who must run a number of ads weekly and who need the resulting work produced quickly. Most other companies are unwisely trying to save 15% of their advertising dollar at the risk of the other 85%. If you want to do your own advertising, I suggest you retain the services of an advertising professional on a consulting basis. Get one who will come to your place of business once a month to look over what you are doing. Agencies charge for consulting on an hourly basis; but, if you get the right advice, it will be worth it.

In *Sales and Marketing Management Magazine,* John M.

Trytten said, "As a rule, the right size agency is the smallest one that can properly handle your account in terms of your budget and the volume of work required."

how agencies charge for their services

Many small advertisers hesitate to retain the services of an advertising agency simply because they have no idea of what the agency might charge. They've heard of the high fees charged by Madison Avenue ad agencies and have equated them with their smaller, local agency counterparts. Or they may have the mistaken impression that agencies are comprised of an assortment of weird "creative" types who charge for their genius like Hollywood superstars.

Advertising agencies are businesses, pure and simple. They have to be fair and reasonable about what they charge for their services. If they charge too much, they won't get enough clients to support them. If they are not businesslike and don't charge enough to cover their expenses and make a profit, they will fail—just like any other business.

Agencies receive the bulk of their income from commissions allowed by media, traditionally 15%. The commission is not a payment to an agency by the media but, rather, a special discount. To be eligible for the media's commission, an agency must meet several criteria: (1) be recognized by media as having business to place, (2) be professionally competent, and (3) be able to meet the financial requirements of the media.

Originally, agencies were not allowed by the media to rebate any portion of these commissions to the client. But, in 1965, the Department of Justice determined that such a restriction was, in effect, a form of price-fixing and therefore illegal. Since then, agencies have been free to rebate part or all of the commissions to their clients, depending on their working arrangement.

Although the commissions received from media are a major source of income for many agencies, they are not always sufficient to cover all expenses incurred in handling a client's advertising. When necessary, an additional fee is charged to the client to make up the difference between the income the agency receives in the form of commissions and the actual costs.

Agencies have a variety of methods for determining a client's fee. The fee may be based on (1) a fixed monthly retainer—estimated on work to be performed plus retention of all commissions received; (2) a fluctuating monthly fee—dependent upon the amount of commissions received by the agency (when commissions are less than an agreed-upon fee, the excess may be credited toward future work for the client); (3) an hourly rate—for services performed to create advertising, such as copywriting and artwork. In this last type of arrangement, the commissions would only cover costs for the time spent in planning, scheduling, billing, and other work involved in handling a client's account—not the creative work.

When there are no commissions available—for producing direct mail or collateral material, for instance—the agency will estimate the project's costs and quote a package price. The quoted price should include all costs for preparing the material and follow-up production.

Most agencies add a service charge to all supplier invoices for outside client expenses, such as typesetting, veloxes, artwork, photography, printing, and so on. All orders are placed by the agency. When bills are received, the agency adds its service charge and then rebills the client.

Any fee arrangement has to be mutually agreed upon between the client and the advertising agency. What is expected of each party should be clearly understood at the very beginning. Is the client to be charged for meetings held at his office to discuss a large campaign, with resulting large commissions? Who will pay for any mistakes, the agency or the client? Will the agency be paid for developing new ideas that may or may not be approved by the client? These are just a few of the points you should consider.

how to select the agency for you

The best way to go about finding the right advertising agency for you is by asking several business friends whom they would recommend. If you're just starting out and don't have anyone to rely on, you'll have to go through the Yellow Pages of the telephone book—look under "Advertising Agencies & Counselors." This is a little like playing Russian roulette, so be careful! First, see if there are any agencies in your immediate area; there's no need to go running all over the county if a good one is close at hand. Select a minimum of three agencies. Arrange an appointment at their offices so you can meet the staff and see their facilities—you can learn a lot by going into a person's place of business. Explain what type of work you think you'll need and ask questions. What services do they provide? How much do they charge for their services? What is their expertise? And so on.

If you run into some sharpie who guarantees advertising results, get out fast; there *ain't no such animal*. Anyone who could guarantee advertising results would be living high on the hog in a New York skyscraper passing judgment on national advertising campaigns.

After you have made the rounds, invite at least two of the prospective agencies to visit your company to meet your people, especially those who will be working directly with the agency.

A few thoughts to keep in mind before you make a decision are the following:

1. Be sure you have a clear understanding as to who will own all of the advertising material produced, you or the agency. As a client, you should insist that all material paid for by you is to be your property.

2. Be certain you don't get stuck with a long-term contract. In most cases, a letter of agreement between you and the agency is sufficient; it should be cancellable on 30 days written notice by either party.

3. Be sure you pick an agency you feel comfortable with and trust, since they will not only be handling large sums of your money but will also come to know many of your company secrets.

Richard Christian, chairman of Marsteller Inc., summed it up in MAC/Western Advertising News. He suggested that clients and agencies have important responsibilities to one another: They include on the part of the agency, giving the client his money's worth, carrying out his objectives, avoiding client politics, becoming immersed in the client's business so as to reinforce the creative process, creating excitement in the client's product or service, and in the marketplace, using the client's money prudently and insuring that the ultimate effort—the advertising itself—appears in print or in broadcast.

"The client's responsibilities," according to Christian, "include providing the advertising funds, protecting such funds from wheeler-dealer sales managers who can always find other uses for the money, providing the agency with access to all levels of corporate executives and communication, inspiring and encouraging agency creativity, demanding proof of results and paying bills on time."*

how to work with your agency

There are also some things you can do for your agency to get maximum benefit from their talents:

1. Don't be a nitpicker. Give your agency its lead. When you feel something is wrong, let your agency people know about it, but don't continually tell them how to do their job.

* From MAC, "Consumer, industrial advertisers borrow creative techniques." Reprinted in SCAN, vol. 25, No. 6, pp. 4–5.

2. Keep the approval system simple. Avoid decision making by committee. It can demoralize an agency and waste a lot of time and money—yours.

3. Be specific about your objectives; let them know they have to produce. If they don't come up with the results you expect after a reasonable time, fire them and hire an agency that can.

4. Do everything you can to assist the agency in learning your business operation. Have the agency account executive come to your office for meetings on a regular basis. If you have more than one store, change the location each time so that the representative can meet more of your people and become familiar with your total operation.

5. Invite the creative team to spend some time at one of your stores on the day of a big sale that they helped to advertise in order to see first hand the results of their efforts. You can be sure the next time they work on one of your sales promotions, they'll work their fannies off.

6. Don't let your personal opinions influence the creative work and selection of media. Your customers' wants, needs, and habits are the primary concern.

7. Don't constantly hassle your agency to buy "cheap." As a businessperson, you know you only "get what you pay for." Give your agency the financial support it needs to present your product in a quality package.

8. Complain when it is necessary, but also be complimentary when it is deserved. Creative people thrive on recognition and will really produce for clients who appreciate their efforts.

9. Be sure your advertising agency makes a profit on your account. The agency should be free of nagging doubts as to whether or not your account is worthwhile handling. This is not a plea for agencies; it's just good business sense. An agency that is well paid will turn itself inside out to give you the best they have in talent and service. And their best efforts will, and should, be reflected in profits for you.

The relationship between advertising agency and client has often been compared to a marriage. And, like any good marriage, it requires a certain amount of give and take by both parties. May you and your agency have many years of "wedded bliss."

THE
ADVERTISING
BUDGET

easy-to-follow rules
for establishing a budget

"If there is any single rule that should dominate the thinking of anyone spending money on advertising or sales promotion, it is: watch every dollar," according to Herschell Gordon Lewis in *The Businessman's Guide to Advertising & Sales Promotions*. And establishing an advertising budget is probably the most important thing you can do to "watch every dollar." It's a good control that allows time for the proper planning and implementation of your total advertising program. It's a guide for evaluating goods and services, a cash flow to pay bills, and a yardstick for measuring the results of the dollars spent.

An ad budget represents the total amount of money a businessperson decides to invest in advertising. Notice that I said "invest," because advertising should be regarded as a long-term investment. And, like any other form of investment, you should logically expect a return. In a *Wall Street Journal* ad, Carl Ally, founder of Carl Ally, Inc., said, ". . . they [clients] know the money they put into advertising comes back to them multiplied. That's what the advertising business is all about. In addition to immediate results, such as sales, advertising has a cumulative effect in terms of benefits—goodwill, company image, and a residual influence on future sales." If you think of advertising as an unwanted expense, you may fritter away your budget; but if you consider it an investment, you will protect that investment, and, properly invested, your advertising dollar will produce profits.

There are a variety of ways to determine how much a company should set aside for advertising purposes. The simplest, and most common, is the "percentage-of-gross-sales" method. It's based on a percentage, usually about 2% to 5%, of a company's gross sales last year. This percentage amount is used for the current year's advertising expenses. A new business, which naturally has no previous sales, would have to base its budget on a percentage of projected sales for the year.

A recent survey indicated that, on an average, small businesses spend 3.1% of gross sales for advertising purposes. Retailers spend an average of 2.5%, whereas service-oriented businesses allocated 3.5%. And businesses with gross sales over $250,000 average 2.5% of the amount for advertising.

For example, let's assume you had gross sales of $400,000 last year. If you decided upon 3% as the amount you could allow for this year's advertising budget, it would come to $12,000. (.03 × $400,000 = $12,000.)

After the budget amount is established, you should prepare a

10

12-month plan for spending the money. Project on a monthly basis, using last year's *monthly* sales figures. Ad expenditures should coincide with periods of high and low sales volumes (see Figures 2–1 and 2–2). According to the Bank of America's *Small Business Reporter*, 'Advertising Small Business,' Vol. 13, No. 8, "The most effective advertising is coordinated with the swings of the business cycle. Advertising expenditures should be higher in the periods when sales are good, enabling the business to capture its full share of the market, and lower when sales are off, so that money will not be wasted on a season with reduced sales potential.

"However, the spending reduction in slack times should not be in direct proportion to the drop in sales. The advertiser must still do a relatively strong job of bidding for a share of the tighter market. Whenever the sales and advertising volumes are not fairly close together, the business is missing opportunities to sell."*

With this in mind, allocate more money for those months when sales are high and less for the months when sales are lower. Plan your

Fig. 2–1 Chart A illustrates the best use of the advertising budget. Advertising expenditures are higher during the months when gross sales figures indicate that business is good; this enables the advertiser to capture his or her full share of the larger market. When gross sales figures drop and business conditions are less attractive, the businessperson reduces the advertising. The reduction is not, however, in direct proportion to the decrease in sales; he or she must still do a relatively strong job of bidding for a share of the difficult-to-obtain market.

CHART A

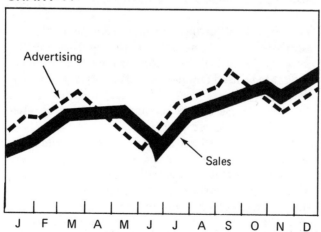

*Reprinted with permission from Bank of America NT & SA, "Advertising Small Business," Vol. 15, No. 2, *Small Business Reporter*, Copyright 1969, 1976, 1978, 1981.

CHART B

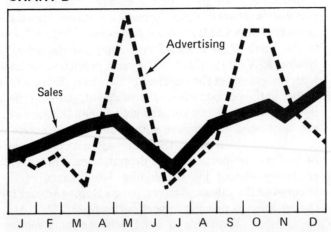

Fig. 2–2 Chart B illustrates bad timing of advertising expenditures. Advertising dollars have been wasted by pouring money into a lagging season and failing to take advantage of a good season.

budget so you'll have more money for advertising when the market is good, such as at Christmas (if you're a retailer); reduce your investment when the market is less favorable. Don't give up advertising altogether during slack periods—it's important to keep your name in the public's mind.

When planning your advertising budget, some practical ideas to remember are the following:

1. Take into consideration holidays, tie-ins with national or local sales promotions, and co-op programs.

2. Allow for a contingency fund of about 5% of the total ad budget to be used for unexpected opportunities and/or new product promotions.

3. Be specific about the amount of advertising dollars to be spent during a given period.

4. Select and schedule carefully from the various media that are available.

5. Watch your costs. Advertising expenditures should normally include costs for media, ad production, and research for testing results. Beware of expenses for miscellaneous items, such as stationery and office forms.

6. Keep your budget flexible: Let the reins out when it's prudent to do so and be prepared, when necessary, to jerk them back quickly.

When preparing a budget, other factors, such as size and type of business, location, competition, profit margin, volume, and long-range plans, all have to be evaluated. The percentage-of-gross-sales method for determining a budget should be regarded as a guide only. But it is a good guide to start with; and, if used wisely, it can help your advertising investment show a profit.

how to estimate
your cost per thousand

"The usual bench mark for comparing costs of comparable media is the cost per thousand circulation of audience," says Otto Kleppner in *Advertising Procedure,* and a knowledge of cost per thousand (CPM) is a must for the advertising person—an invaluable tool for use in establishing future budgets. If you are doing some form of advertising and don't know, or only have a vague idea of, how to calculate CPM's, make yourself comfortable and read on slowly.

Cost per thousand, or CPM, as it is commonly referred to, is the most used common denominator to determine how much it would cost an advertiser to reach 1,000 people through a given medium.

To calculate CPM's, you simply divide the circulation figure of the medium into the cost of the ad (in magazines it's based on a full-page, black-and-white ad, at the one-time rate). Round off the circulation figure to the nearest thousand and drop the last three zeros; it'll make the math easier. For example, if you are considering a publication with a circulation of 24,000 readers and the ad insertion cost is $720, the CPM would be $30 ($720 ÷ 24 = $30).

Let's try another one. Imagine that your advertising message is to appear in a magazine with a circulation of 1,000 and that the cost of the space is $150: The CPM is simply $150. You would pay $150 to reach 1,000 people. Now suppose you can run the same ad in a different publication that also charges $150 but has a circulation of 2,000. In this case your CPM would be $75 ($150 ÷ 2 = $75). If you had to make a decision on which medium to use, based on cost alone, the answer is obvious—the second publication with the lower CPM is your best buy.

Just to make sure you have the hang of it, let me give you some sample problems to figure out by yourself. Don't panic: They're easy and only take a few seconds. Remember the formula: ad cost divided by circulation = CPM. The answers are at the end of this chapter, but don't look before you have finished. Try them.

Problem 1. $690 \div 24 =$ CPM
Problem 2. $595 \div 10 =$ CPM
Problem 3. $460 \div 20 =$ CPM

If you were trying to reach a special group like left-handed brain surgeons, then you would simply advertise in the "Left-Handed Brain Surgeons Gazette," if it were the only publication available. You wouldn't have to worry about CPM's. But if there were two magazines read by left-handed brain surgeons, then CPM's would tell you which of the two is more economical.

The CPM formula can also be used to compare advertising costs between different media. But remember, compare magazines with magazines and newspapers with newspapers—don't try comparing "apples with oranges."

In electronic media, such as radio and television, audiences are based on Gross Rating Points (GRP) and/or the Cumulative Audience (Cumes). Audience figures are calculated and adjusted in such a complicated manner that they are not only bewildering to the beginner but difficult for the professional to understand and use intelligently. You can use the CPM method of comparison with the broadcast media if you again remember to compare apples with apples—the same length commercials at the same time period of a given day.

What about direct mail? Well, if you consider CPM's alone, direct mail is an expensive way to advertise. A CPM based on the cost of first-class postage alone comes to $180. That's right, based on 1981 postage rates, the 18¢ stamp for a mailing of 1,000 pieces adds up to $180. And bulk mail is not cheap either: At the 1981 bulk rate of 10.4¢, the CPM comes to $104—for junk mail.

Don't forget that the CPM is based only on the total number of people who will be exposed to your message. It does not gauge how many of them will actually see or read it. There are other factors you should be aware of when determining which medium you should use. The size or length, copy message, design, use of color, placement, and date of appearance of your ad can all affect response.

spend your money wisely— the right place and time

Every year millions of dollars say "goodbye" to advertisers who select their media with carefree abandon. The decision is based on expediency or emotion, as opposed to careful consideration.

Let me give you an example. One day a client phoned to proudly announce he had just signed a season contract for advertising space on the local baseball scoreboard. If he were selling hot dogs, soft drinks, or promoting an after-game beer joint, it would have made some sense. However, he sold office products—not just ordinary supplies but rather sophisticated office equipment. I explained to him that people attending a sports event were there to be entertained and that his money would have been better spent in a more practical medium. But it was too late: The contract was noncancellable, and the advertising ran its course with predictable results—none.

Unfortunately, this situation is fairly common among advertisers; they get arm-twisted into a medium they don't belong in and end up convinced that "advertising doesn't work."

Advertising does work, but the best ad in the world will not pull if it is placed in the wrong medium. Would girdles sell if they were displayed in the men's section of a department store? Of course not; they are in the wrong place, appealing to the wrong type of person. So it is with advertising. To be effective, your message has to appear in the right medium, appealing to the person who may logically be interested in your product. How often have you heard the old adage about "being in the right place at the right time?" Likewise, your advertising message should be in the right medium at the right time.

Careful screening and selection of the available media are absolutely essential to the success of your advertising efforts.

To determine which medium is the right one for you, it's important to be able to define your potential customers. Be specific. Identify them as to age, sex, occupation, income, and so on. Most media have demographic studies identifying their readers or listeners. Get a copy of these studies from each medium you are considering. Compare them to decide which media are directed toward the same type of people you are trying to reach—at the lowest cost. Media representatives, suppliers, trade associations, and trade publications are all good sources of this type of information. Just remember that the information they supply is self-serving and is best taken with a grain of salt.

Once you have established who your customers are and where you can reach them, you'll have to assess the best time to reach them. Weekly? Monthly? Seasonally? Yearly? "A blunderer is a man who starts a meat market during Lent," said James Montgomery Bailey. Don't be a blunderer.

Try to anticipate customer needs in advance. Plan for special events and holidays when prospective customers will be interested in what you have to sell. For example, supermarkets heavily promote hamburgers, buns, soft drinks, charcoal briquets, etc. just before a holiday week-end when people will be looking for and buying picnic items. The Monday after the weekend is obviously too late.

six things *not* to do

Here are a few "don'ts" that will help keep you from drifting off course:

1. Don't spread your ad budget too thin by trying to be in a lot of different publications. No advertiser can afford to use all the various media constantly urged upon him or her. Pick primary and secondary media; then pour your ad bucks into them: You'll build consistency, recognition, and impact. In addition, you'll benefit by getting better rate discounts.

2. Don't sign any media contract until you have had time to evaluate it and until you are certain the cost is within your advertising budget.

3. Don't purchase advertising space or time only in media you like. Your customers' reading and listening habits should be the number one consideration.

4. Don't jump into the first issue of a new publication; the failure rate is too high. Wait until the publication is established before you decide if it's for you. Keep your advertising dollars in proven media—where they will work for you.

5. Don't fall for high-pressure sales pitches from space or time salespeople. Tell them your budget is set and that the ad schedule is closed. Suggest they come back in six months—most of them won't.

6. Don't get stuck advertising in every program, bulletin, and so on that is forced on you. They usually won't pull.

Don't forget what I just said.

stretching an ad budget
with co-op funds

One of the first jobs I had in advertising was to prepare full-page news-paper ads for some local food-market clients. My primary responsibility was to crank out page after page of advertising featuring the latest sale prices for such items as Dole pineapple juice (46 oz.), Hunt's tomato sauce (12 oz. can), Ivory soap (large size), Maxwell House coffee (1 lb.), Camp-bell's soups (tomato), and literally hundreds of similar products. Some-where along the line my curiosity got the best of me, and I asked my boss how these relatively small food markets could afford the tremendous amount of advertising they were doing every week. The eye-opening answer was, "Cooperative Advertising." It's a way you, an advertiser with a small ad budget, can increase your advertising efforts.

It has been estimated by various sources that more than half of the department-store advertising done in this country is on a cooperative basis and that the investment in co-op advertising is between three and four billion dollars annually.

Co-op advertising is that form of advertising that features a brand-name product and is placed in a local medium by a retailer—the costs are then shared by both the retailer and manufacturer. In some cooperative programs, the advertising costs are also shared by the distributor and the wholesaler. The amount shared is usually, but not always, on a 50/50 basis. The Federal Robinson-Patman Act governs cooperative advertising and requires manufacturers who offer a co-op program to make the same opportunities, or percentages of reimbursement, available to all dealers selling their products.

Manufacturers set aside funds for retailers to use for co-op advertising of the manufacturer's product that are based either on a certain percentage of dealer sales or on a per-product (unit) amount. A yearly or seasonal limit on the total funds available is established, depending on the dealer's volume of sales.

Many manufacturers establish restrictions as to how the co-op money is to be used; sometimes the medium to run the advertising in is specified in the program. Although newspapers make up the bulk of co-op advertising, other media, such as magazines, radio, television, and direct mail, may also be included.

Some manufacturers require a participating dealer to use specially prepared ad material, brand logos, illustrations; or they may specify the exact wording to appear in a co-op ad. Most manufacturers supply professionally prepared newspaper ad mats, television videotape, direct mail pieces, radio scripts, and recordings for the retailer's use. In all of the material provided, room is allowed to insert the dealer's store name and other pertinent information.

Prior approval, from the manufacturer, of an ad that is prepared by the dealer is necessary in certain situations, particularly with retailers using co-op funds for the first time.

Manufacturers normally give advance notification to the dealer of national advertising promotions planned for their products. This allows the dealer time to stock additional inventory and to make arrangements to use advertising that will tie in with the manufacturer's efforts in order to gain maximum sales benefits.

A retailer, if permitted, may use the co-op funds of different manufacturers to create a large "omnibus" type of ad, charging each manufacturer a proportionate share of the total cost. In this type of ad, each portion of the ad allocated for a product should be defined with borders so that the space can be easily and accurately measured.

Reimbursement from the manufacturer, by cash or credit memo, is dependent on proof of performance by the retailer in the form of duplicate media invoices accompanied by a copy of the ad. For newspaper and magazine advertising, a tearsheet is supplied; radio and television commercials require a station affidavit of performance.

If you are interested in participating in a cooperative advertising program, be sure to ask the manufacturer's sales representative the following questions:

1. What amount of purchases will you be required to make?
2. What percentage is paid on the purchase amount?
3. What portion will the manufacturer pay for advertising?
4. What are the restrictions imposed?
5. What are your obligations?

It's vital to know what's expected of you *before* you take part in a co-op program. A few other things I strongly suggest you be sure to do before you sign any agreement are these:

1. Get and read a free copy of "Advertising Allowances and Other Merchandising Programs" from the Division of Legal & Public Records, Federal Trade Commission, Washington, D.C. 20580.
2. Understand the program you are considering completely.
3. Have the manufacturer's sales representative confirm that funds have been accrued and are available for your use.

Properly used, co-op advertising can help you in several ways. First, you can increase your store's prestige by being identified with a national brand-name product. Second, by adding co-op dollars to your ad budget, you will become eligible for larger volume discounts offered by media, stretching your ad dollars further. Third, you will generate store traffic. The advertising of brand-name products brings customers in, and that, in turn, will increase your sales of other merchandise.

Oh, yes, the CPM problems; here are the answers: (1) $28.75; (2) $59.50; (3) $23.

COPYWRITING

a.i.d.a., a simple formula
to get you started

There comes a time in everyone's advertising life when you are asked to write an advertisement and your mind goes absolutely, totally blank. Drained of inspiration, all you are able to do is stare at a piece of white paper lying in front of you. The deadline to have the ad ready hangs over your head like a swinging sword, slowly descending, ready to give it to you in the neck. At a time like this you wonder how you ever got into this crazy business, and why you didn't take up something less demanding, such as brain surgery. It happens to all of us. Famed adman Leo Burnett knows how it feels. He said, "Probably nothing was ever more bleak. . . . Out of the recesses of his [the copywriter's] mind must come words which interest, words which persuade, words which inspire, words which sell."

When you're in this kind of bind, it's a great temptation to reach for the old clichés, grab the familiar advertising buzz words, or clutch for a bunch of puffed-up superlatives. It's the lazy way out. Don't give in to temptation.

When the going gets tough, it's time to go back to basics. Advertising pros do; and they use a simple, classic formula for writing copy that enables them to get the juices flowing again: It's called "A.I.D.A." A.I.D.A. stands for Attention, Interest, Desire, and Action.

A.I.D.A. is not the only formula for writing an ad—far from it. It is not a rigid rule. It is also not a crutch for lazy copywriting. It is an ice-breaker that can help crack that barren expanse of white paper and get you started writing an ad that has attention, interest, desire, and action.

Here's how it works.

Attention (headline): You start by getting attention in the headline. Attention that will attract the reader not only to read the headline but also slowly to pull him or her into reading the entire ad like a magnet. There are different attention-getting approaches you can use. The one I find to be most effective is to promise the reader a strong benefit; a benefit that will satisfy one of the basic needs for well-being. Thomas D. Murray, Murray and Chaney Advertising, Hudson, Ohio, hit the nail on the head when he said, "People do not pay attention to advertising; they pay attention to what interests them."

There's no better way of stimulating interest in your product than by appealing to the reader's self-interest. The average ad reader wants to know what your product can do for him or her. How will it further his well-being? Why should he read your ad? In short, what's in it for him?

20

A very important factor to consider in writing the headline is to write it from the reader's point of view, not yours. Advertising writer Kenneth M. Goode said, "Don't tell people how good you make your products. Tell people how good your products make them." Advertisements that promise a benefit to the reader sell more than those that don't. But be sure your claims are not only valid but credible; offer proof whenever possible. It is important that the product fulfills the promise, whatever that promise may be (the FTC, FDA, etc. might ask you for substantiation).

How important is an attention-getting headline? Well, an ad that doesn't attract attention doesn't get read. It's worse than useless.

Interest (subheadline): Okay, you've gained the reader's attention; now you have to elaborate on the benefit you promised. Don't be general or vague. Be specific and continue to follow through on the single idea with which you started. Add to it. Support it with more information on the importance of the benefit. Get the reader involved. Give him a solid reason to read further. Make him feel that he will miss something important (again to him, not to you) if he doesn't continue reading.

Try to use magic words (if appropriate), such as "new," "introducing," "suddenly," "now just arrived," "improved," "free," and "newly developed," when writing your subheadlines. They are definite eye-grabbers.

Desire (text, also called the "body copy"): In the headline, you got attention by promising a benefit. In the subhead, you created further interest in the promise. Now you have to convince the customer he wants the product you are offering.

Appeal to the reader on a one-to-one basis. Imagine you are talking to a friend, trying to tell him why he should buy your product. Talk directly to the reader as if he were a real person—someone you know. Write in the same language you would use in speaking, language that is easily understood. Make the wording difficult to understand, or insult the reader's intelligence, and you've lost him. " 'Cease motion, observe carefully and note sound of approaching train', can't compare with 'Stop, Look and Listen'," said John Pullen, in *Printer's Ink*.

Use a personal approach in your copy with words such as "you," "yours," "yourself," and "you too." Keep "I," "me," "we," "our," and the like to a minimum. Although you may be reaching thousands of people with your message, write it as if you're speaking to only one—the reader.

The body copy can be long or short, depending on how much

information the reader needs in order to make a buying decision. Just be sure it is factual, informative, and imaginative: You can't be boring and still persuade a customer to buy your product. And the customer, of course, is you and me and people like us—don't ever forget it.

Be to the point and be clear. The reader has neither the time nor patience to unscramble some obscure meaning you are trying to get across, no matter how clever it may be.

You can be effective by using short, simple words, phrases, and sentences and by eliminating words that do not add to the clarity of the message. Don't brag or boast; nobody likes a braggart. Get your imaginary friend enthusiastic about the product: The best way to do that is to be enthusiastic yourself and reflect that feeling in the copy you write. You have to create a desire that is strong enough to motivate him to go out and fork over his hard-earned money for the product. It's not easy, but you can do it.

Action (closing): Surprisingly, this is the point at which many ads go limp and collapse. It's the time to "ask for the order." Every good salesperson knows this; hasn't advertising been referred to as "salesmanship in print?" Just as a good salesperson, upon completion of the sales presentation, whips out the order book and asks the customer to sign on the dotted line, so must you remember to ask the reader to "get one today" or "send in the coupon," or "visit one of our conveniently located stores." Study some mail-order ads; you will find that no matter how small the ad, there is always a call to action. Over the years, mail-order advertisers have learned that if you don't get the customer to take prompt action ("Order now!", "Don't delay . . ."), he or she will procrastinate and inevitably forget you and your advertisement.

That's A.I.D.A.—a simple, easy-to-follow formula for writing an ad. It beats staring at blank paper, drinking three pots of coffee, or running around the block to get started.

A.I.D.A. will help you write your ad; but before you even think about writing, gather all the facts you can about the product. If possible, use the product and become familiar with it. Determine its unique selling feature. In other words, find out what makes it different and better than other, similar products. Effective copy is the result of product knowledge, reader research, and good, old-fashioned hard work.

And as you start writing, always keep in mind advertising's prime rule: Keep it simple.

helpful hints for headlines

David Ogilvy, in *Confessions of an Advertising Man*, noted, "On the average, five times as many people read the headline as read the body copy. When you have written your headline, you have spent eighty cents of your dollar. If you haven't done some selling in your headline, you have wasted 80% of your client's money."

The headline should be designed to grab the reader's attention, hold interest, and slowly but surely lure him or her into reading the rest of the ad. Its job is to sell the product or service being advertised, not merely to entertain the reader or, worse, massage the copywriter's ego.

A good headline should make people read, understand, believe, and desire your product or service. If the headline fails, chances are the reader will ignore your ad—the worst insult that can be inflicted on an advertiser.

To attract the busy reader who is flipping through a publication, your words must be very compelling. They should reach out and say, in effect, "Stop! Read this, it's important to your well-being."

Here are a few tips to help you when you write a headline:

1. Start by jotting down all of the headline possibilities you can think of—even the bad ones (get them out of your system). Write and rewrite the same general idea in many different ways. Don't be concerned about length, but do eliminate needless words. Say what you have to, then stop.

2. When possible, include your company or product name.

3. Avoid negative words; people tend to remember them associated with your product.

4. If the ad is for a special group, such as balding men or overweight people, say so.

5. Don't use advertising clichés, such as "Best in the West," or "It's a hit!" They, and too many more like them, are just too trite to be believed.

6. Write more than one headline. Try several approaches from different angles.

Select the best of your ideas, then polish, refine, and rework the little gem until it is as original and persuasive as you can make it.

Once you have a really good headline, the rest of the copywriting task will be less difficult. In fact, it's much easier to write copy to match a headline than it is to try to write a headline that will match the body copy.

types of headlines

Headlines usually, but not always, fall into one of the following categories. Don't let your thinking be restricted by these categories, however, since many successful headlines combine two or more of the approaches.

Benefit Headline: People want to know about products that will help make them healthier, wealthier, wiser, and so on. If your product offers a real benefit, let your customers know about it. Present the benefit clearly in a few well-chosen words, such as "Datsun's new B-210 gives you a nifty fifty (mpg)." Remember, any claims you make have to be backed up with proof.

Straightforward Headline: A simple statement about the product and its quality, use, or importance (to the reader). It's more of a slogan than a headline and needs to be supported by frequent exposure over a long period of time. "Come to Marlboro country" is typical.

News Headline: The consumer is always on the lookout for new ideas, products, or uses for established products. Your product is only new once, so make the most of it. The magic words—"New," "Now," "Introducing," "At last . . . ," and so on—are good to use. Some examples are, "New paper towels are more absorbent" and "Now, you can get these two great Chunky Soups in a single-serving size."

Storytelling Headline: Appeals to people who are intrigued by a statement that promises to lead them into a story. "They all laughed when I sat down to play the piano" is a classic example. But unless you're really expert at it, don't try this approach.

Advice Headline: This type of headline offers the reader help in making purchases or solving a problem. "Here are 13 new ways to prepare hamburgers" and "How to reduce energy costs in your home" are different ways to do it.

Questioning Headline: A question is presented in the headline to arouse the reader's curiosity and encourage the reading of the rest of the ad. Be sure you satisfy that curiosity, or the reader will feel tricked. One of the most successful ads ever created asked, "Do you make these common mistakes in English?"

Selective Headline: The reader is more likely to read a headline when it directly relates to his or her needs. With these problems, who could resist, "Hemorrhoid sufferers: Get soothing relief, fast . . .," or "Do you have itchy, flaky dandruff. . . ."

If you're in doubt as to how to get started, try the first approach—the reader benefit-oriented headline. Ogilvy said, "Headlines that promise a benefit sell more than those that don't."

Also, resist the temptation to be clever at the expense of your sales message. As I've said before, stay away from advertising clichés and buzz words. Your headline might not be as catchy as that rare, creative gem that lights up the advertising sky; but, in most instances, it will impress people enough to make them go out and buy your product. And isn't that what you really want to accomplish?

successful selling with "sale" ads

Advertising should sell; on this, we all agree. A retailer often wants to sell a "sale," so let's spend a few minutes talking about "sale ads."

If you're a retailer and are planning a sale, newspapers are the most effective medium to use. When it comes to actually bringing customers into the store, no other medium can compare with them. "The reason people use newspaper is because it sells. . . . When you run a good newspaper ad you move merchandise," says Henry Katz of Lorrilard & Company.

When you're planning your sale ad, keep the following in mind:

1. Phony discounts of 10% to 50% are pretty common in today's marketplace. If you want to avoid the reputation of a cut-rate operation, be sure you are offering a legitimate bargain before you start.

2. To get the maximum impact for your promotion, feature the word "sale" as large as possible in your advertising. Remember, it's a "magic" word, so don't whisper, shout! Big is beautiful.

3. Don't let the theme of the sale override the fact that you are having one. "Welcome back springtime sale" or "We're having a happy

ground hog day sale" can get in the way. Be specific about the type of sale you are promoting.

4. Generalized copy claims are a common weakness in advertising; they are usually the result of laziness on the part of the writer. To paraphrase the well-known adage, "Good copy is 90% perspiration and only 10% inspiration."

5. If you're concerned about your store's image—and you should be—sale ads can be done in good taste. It takes some imagination and effort, but you can do it. Just make certain present and potential customers know you are having a sale. Soft-sell is nice, but sell-sell is better.

6. The headline should grab attention and interest the reader enough to continue reading the rest of the ad to find out what items are on sale. Keep your body copy relatively brief; go easy on the prose and heavy on the information the reader needs. Colors, sizes, fabrics, availabilities of items, and the like will influence the reader in making a decision to purchase.

7. Unbelievable as it may sound, many ads fail to include the store's location—don't make this mistake. It's presumptuous of an advertiser to assume that everyone knows where all of his or her stores are located. Recent figures show that almost one-third of the American people are changing addresses annually. Out-of-town visitors and new residents don't know where you are, and present customers have to be continually reminded. Make it easy for your customers; spell out your location(s).

8. Along with your address, include the store hours, the dates of the sale, the credit cards you accept, parking availability, and so on. It can be in small type if space is a problem, but be sure to include this information.

9. Next in importance to the headline in getting the reader's attention is the illustration of the advertised product. Use illustrations that are attractive and professional. Most manufacturers supply good quality artwork of their products—for free. If they meet your needs, use them.

10. Photos in newspapers do not, as a rule, reproduce well. If you use a photo, be sure it has good contrast—strong black and white areas. Photos with a lot of middle tones tend to soften and lose detail.

11. A good way to announce a sale to current customers is through your monthly statements. Simply give them an advance announcement about the sale. They're prime prospects, and the cost will be low since you already will have paid for the envelope and postage.

12. Have removable SALE signs put on company trucks. They become, in effect, low-cost moving billboards, announcing the sale wherever they go.

13. Follow up sale ads by decorating your store(s) inside and outside with SALE banners, SALE posters, SALE displays, SALE price tags, and so on. Now reread this paragraph. Is there any doubt I am talking about a sale? You should do the same thing.

plan a campaign, not a skirmish

Just as the politician has to plan, coordinate, and implement a campaign to win votes, so must the advertiser think in terms of a "campaign" to win customer approval.

An advertising campaign is a series of different ads related by the same ongoing theme. The theme can be in many forms—a distinctive copy approach, an art style, an ad format, a jingle, a slogan, a spokesperson, or any combination of these elements.

People are busy and tend to forget things rather readily, especially advertising. Quick: Can you name a television commercial you saw last night? If you're typical of most people, you probably can't. An advertising campaign, through sheer force of frequency and repetition of appearance, keeps the public constantly reminded of a product or service. And ads that are a part of a total campaign have a greater synergistic effect than the same number of single, nonrelated ads—it's an extra benefit for which you don't have to pay. In addition, campaigns can be very cost effective compared to the expense involved in constantly changing individual ads. With a campaign, you can repeat artwork, format, borders, photography, typography, and so on: It's a great way to amortize production costs, and you should take advantage of it.

Plan your campaign months ahead in order to eliminate the need to rush through ads at the last minute. Agree, in advance, with your advertising agency on specific, realistic marketing goals and the strategy that will be employed to reach them.

Be sure you budget enough money to do the total job; it's painful to plan a trip and wind up with only enough money to get half-way to your destination.

Your campaign should be a totally integrated effort. The central theme or visual device should be incorporated in all forms of advertising, such as newspapers, magazines, radio, and television. It should be easily identifiable wherever it appears: All in-store signs, displays, banners, buttons, and the like should carry the same message. This is called the "total look," and it adds recall value to the campaign.

Different ads might be needed within a campaign, appealing to various types of consumer groups while still maintaining the central theme. For instance, a department store might promote a sale of inexpensive plastic dishware in one ad and in the following ad offer an expensive piece of jewelry at the regular price. In both cases, however, the underlying theme of the campaign would point out the quality of all merchandise sold in the store, regardless of price.

Campaigns can be used for promoting general merchandise on a regular weekly, monthly, or quarterly basis and/or to cover special sales events, such as holidays, clearances, and semi-annual sales.

Consumer attitudes, needs, fashions, and fads are always changing. To keep in tune with the times, ad campaigns, like any form of advertising, have to be continually monitored, evaluated, and revised when there is a need. Changes in the competition's marketing program, a modification in the present product, or the introduction of a new product can affect your selling effort. It pays to find out what the real reasons are for lagging sales before you drastically revise a proven campaign. Don't blame advertising without doing some research.

An institutional campaign can be very effective for an advertiser who wishes to build goodwill, recognition, or confidence in a store or product. Institutional ads do not sell merchandise but, rather, promote image-building concepts, such as experience—"The world's most experienced airline"; professionalism—"The quality goes in before the name goes on"; dependability—"You can be sure if it's Westinghouse"; or integrity—"You have our word on it."

Surprisingly, some advertisers discard an advertising campaign while it is still doing well. Why? Simply because they have grown "tired of it" and mistakenly think the public has too. These are the same people who would never think of leaving a slot machine during a hot streak, but they'll scrap a successful campaign before it is worn out. Resist the temptation. A good advertising campaign can run successfully for years. And it will certainly cost you less money than it would to come up with new ads again and again.

On the surface, a campaign may seem like a major undertaking, but it really isn't. In fact, a good, coordinated campaign is much easier to produce than a series of different ads. By using a campaign approach, you can focus all of your energy and creative juices on the single, most effective method to communicate an idea; once you have that, everything else will fall into place quickly.

preparing your copy for production

After you've incorporated the basic fundamentals of copywriting and come up with an ad that says what you want to say, you're ready to put your copy into a final form. Now, how would you like to save some of your advertising dollars? It's very easy; all you have to do is take time to read all of your advertising copy carefully before you approve it for production. Sounds simple, doesn't it? It is, yet thousands of ad dollars are wasted each year because advertisers don't take the time to read their copy seriously when they should—at the beginning. As a result, incorrect information, prices, phone numbers, and the like have to be changed in the final stages of production, a costly and needless expense. In the words of J. Jenkins, "To err is human, but when the eraser wears out ahead of the pencil, you're overdoing it." If errors are caught in the early stages of production, they cost nothing, or very little, to correct. Let me explain.

After advertising copy has been approved, the next step is to have it set in type. Typesetting is that part of the ad production process dealing with the selection and arrangement of type.

Typesetters base their charges on the time it takes them to set copy in type. For this reason, your copy should always be submitted in typewritten form. Handwritten copy can be very difficult to read at times; and if a typesetter has to slowly decipher poorly handwritten material, it will cost more. Also, poor handwriting can cause errors that will have to be redone; this can get extremely expensive—again depending at what stage the errors are noted and corrected.

Here's what you should do to help keep your costs down.

Before sending any copy to a typesetter, have it typed, double-spaced, on one side of a sheet of plain, white paper (8½ × 11 inches); the company stationery is ideal for this purpose. In the upper left-hand corner of each sheet, indicate the appropriate page number to avoid having pages handled out of sequence. On pages where the copy is to be continued, put the word "more" at the bottom of the page. On the last page, to show that the copy is completed, use the proofreader's symbol "#", centered two spaces below the last line. Double-spacing the typewritten lines makes them easier to read and also allows room for minor revisions to be made without retyping the entire page. If the necessary revisions cover a paragraph or more, the changes can be retyped on another sheet and taped over the original copy. If, after all the revisions are made, the copy sheet suddenly resembles a Chinese railroad map, I suggest you have the whole page neatly retyped. It will cost a lot less in the long run.

Edit your copy carefully. Changes should be made at the typewritten, rather than the typeset, stage. After your copy is typeset, a simple, single-letter change will necessitate having the whole line reset. And when the change is a word, it could lead to having the entire paragraph done over. After the material has been set in type, revisions become "Author's Alterations," and then things become expensive. The cost to make "AA's" is billed to the client at a much higher rate than for the original copy. Some typesetting companies have a standard charge of $1 per line to reset new copy, which gives you a rough idea of how costly these corrections can get. Charging a higher rate for author's alterations is an industry-wide practice, established to discourage people from making endless changes. Try to keep your author's alterations to an absolute minimum to avoid rapidly escalating typesetting costs.

Typesetters make errors, too. A typesetter's mistake is called a "typo," and the client should not be charged for having this kind of correction made.

Proofreaders' marks (see Figure 3–1) are used for indicating instructions or changes to be made in copy. Everyone working with type—ad agencies, newspapers, book publishers, and so on—use this standard form of shorthand. You can get a copy of proofreader's marks from any typesetter or from your local newspaper sales representative or you can find a list of them in most dictionaries. Although it is a good idea for the beginner to be familiar with some of the more common proofreader's marks, it is not absolutely necessary. Clear, simple English serves the same purpose.

After the copy has been set in the desired type style(s), you will be supplied with at least two typeset sheets, called "proofs." One is usually of poor quality and is used to check the copy to make sure it is as ordered; it's called a "Rough" or "Reader" proof. The other is of excellent quality: Its purpose is to be pasted in artwork and used for reproduction; it's appropriately called a "Repro" proof. Some typesetters can supply repro proofs with an adhesive wax backing on the paper that makes them easy to mount in artwork. The rough proof should be carefully read for punctuation, spelling, typographic errors, and particularly for accuracy. It's not uncommon to get the message 100% perfect, only to later find an error in the company's address or phone number—an unpardonable sin.

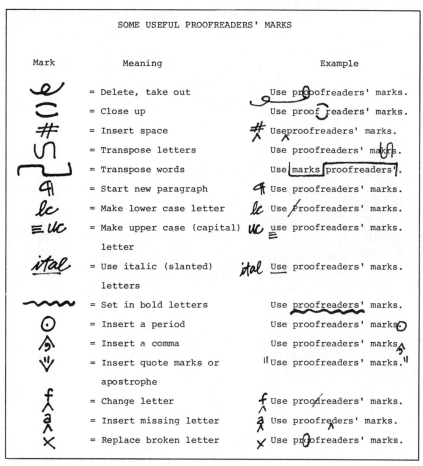

Fig. 3-1 Some useful proofreaders' marks.

There are several ways to get your message set in type. Copy can be set in type by the local publications in which the ad is to appear, usually without charge, or by typesetting companies that specialize in this work. They are listed in the Yellow Pages of the telephone book under "Typesetting."

If you remember to follow these simple steps, you'll save some of your advertising money.

1. Type your copy on white paper, double-spaced.
2. Read it over very carefully and make any necessary changes before sending it to the typesetter.

3. Reread it when you receive the finished form from the type-setter.

These are the basic elements of copywriting, from the beginning idea to the finished form for reproduction. Keep these guidelines in mind; they'll help you through the maze of ad writing.

ARTWORK

commercial artists—
creative communicators

Commercial artists are talented, sensitive, prideful, shy, arrogant, frustrating, emotional, lovable, and wonderfully crazy people. If you have ever worked with one of them, you know what I mean.

But even with all of their idiosyncrasies, they are still indispensable members of the advertising team. A professional artist can sometimes see sales features you may have overlooked and provide fresh insights that can bring out that something special, that something different that makes your product stand out from the crowd of competition. "Creativeness often consists of merely turning up what is already there," noted Bernice Fitz-Gibbon. An experienced professional artist can design an advertisement, mailing piece, or booklet with such visual impact that it can penetrate reader indifference and ring cash registers.

Who are these illustrative idea people? Commercial artists, sometimes referred to as graphic designers or simply as designers, can be found in the art departments of advertising agencies, art studios, film studios, department stores, and companies that have a need for artwork. Self-employed commercial artists, known as "free-lancers," usually work at home. You can find them listed in the Yellow Pages under "Artists, Commercial."

Artists may specialize in one or more of the following areas: illustration, advertising layout, graphic design, paste-up, mechanical drawing, lettering, retouching, package design, signs, posters, cartooning, record-album jackets, and book-cover design. There is a wealth of artistic talent available to fit any need.

How do you select an artist? Professional artists have samples of their work in a holder or binder called a portfolio. It usually contains about a dozen examples of the artist's work, enough to help you decide if the person has the necessary ability to do your job. Never, never hire an artist you don't know without first looking at his or her portfolio. The artist can have a stack of college degrees and talk until blue in the face about creative abilities; but if he or she doesn't have samples of some recent work, you'll be buying the proverbial pig-in-a-poke.

Because of their diverse talent and experience, there are no standard fees charged by artists. Rates are based on what they feel their talent is worth, plus the value of the job assignment. A word of caution: A low rate does not necessarily mean you'll save money. An inexperienced artist who is not familiar with properly preparing artwork for reproduction can increase printing costs, particularly in color work. For example, an artist should know how to "gang-up" color photos to reduce the number of

34

individual color separations on a four-color printing job. If the artist doesn't know how to do this, the budget can go through the ceiling.

When discussing rates with an artist, ask for a total package price. The price should include all costs for the artist's work, such as layouts, illustrations, and paste-ups, plus outside costs for typography, photography, veloxes, stats, and prints. When a firm package price is established, it then becomes the responsibility of the artist to stay within the budget. Expect to pay half of the fee before the job is begun, with the balance due upon completion and acceptance of the finished work.

Prior to reaching an agreement, be sure you have an understanding as to who owns the final artwork, you or the artist. Some artists sell first rights to their work and maintain ownership, even though you pay for it. The time to establish that you retain ownership of the artwork is at the beginning, when the artist is anxious to get the job. After the work is finished may be too late.

Before an assignment is begun, explain to the artist, as fully as you can, what your ideas are, what type of artwork you need, and the reason you need it. Giving the artist your input establishes a direction for the job.

When the finished, camera-ready artwork is submitted to you for approval, look it over very carefully. Accuracy in the final product is your responsibility. Read every word, every digit, and every comma in the copy. Don't be rushed; make sure it is absolutely correct. You don't want your piece to appear in print only to find that the address or phone number is incorrect. Also, double check the measurements of the artwork; be certain they are accurate. If a mailer is off size by as little as one-quarter of an inch, it might not fit into the envelope designed for it.

After the piece has been printed, be sure the original artwork is returned to you, and then save it. You'll find all or some portions of it can be used again. Artwork can be enlarged, reduced, or recropped and used in new booklets, ads, mailers, and so on. Maintain a good filing system for all of your artwork, photographs, and even type proofs. You'll be pleasantly surprised at what you can recycle.

layout—your advertising blueprint

Creating an advertising layout is somewhat like trying to put together a jigsaw puzzle. You have a collection of different pieces (ad elements) that must fit together in order to form a completed (ad) picture. If you have too many pieces, pieces that don't belong, or pieces that don't fit properly, it just won't come out right. But when you have the right combination of pieces and assemble them correctly, they will form the total picture you want your readers to see.

The key to designing an attractive, attention-getting ad is simplicity. In the words of Tony Majeri of the *Chicago Tribune*, "Never let the layout get in the way of the reader. Be a little conservative rather than a little too cute." Unfortunately, many beginners throw everything they can into an ad because "the space is paid for anyway." As a result, the ad resembles the aftermath of Hurricane Hilda. It's visual pollution or worse, because it doesn't help the advertiser sell.

As an advertiser, you should be aware of the "making of an ad." And by understanding what goes into your ad, you will be able to improve its effectiveness.

The basic elements of an ad layout are the headline, the illustration or photograph, the copy, and the advertiser's signature. Other elements, such as subheadings, lists, and coupons, are sometimes included. The importance of an element determines its size and placement within the ad.

The "layout" is the visual blueprint of an ad or printed piece. It is used to show the advertiser how the finished ad will look. After the advertiser has approved the layout, it becomes a guide for the production of the finished artwork. Copy will be measured and type set to fit the copy areas. Illustrations, hand lettering, or photography can be ordered using the layout as a reference for size, style, and content.

The artist's task is to select the most important feature of the advertiser's product or service and design an ad that will emphasize that characteristic. For instance, if the product advantage is size, the layout should show it in proportion to other similar products.

The headline and/or photo is usually featured and deserves the most conspicuous position in the layout—at the top of the page. Provide adequate space to make it big enough to dominate the other parts of the ad.

Lead the reader's eye from your headline and/or photo quickly and smoothly through the ad from one element to the next in a logical, easy-to-follow visual path. This visual flow should interest and encourage the reader to see and read the most important feature first, then move to the secondary piece of information, and onward through the entire ad without stopping. Otto Kleppner, in the sixth edition of *Advertising Procedure*, likened the elements to visual "stepping stones." If the reader wanders from the path you've established, he or she will lose interest and turn the page.

The layout should attract favorable attention. But attention for attention's sake is not enough. It's pretty easy to get the reader's attention—just have a picture of a nude person holding your product. What really gets the attention and is remembered? You guessed it. Roy Durstine, BBD&O Advertising, said, "The most important job of an advertisement is to center all the attention on the merchandise and none on the technique of presenting it."

A well-designed ad will have (1) balance, (2) flow, and (3) unity. Balance, whether formal or informal, will keep the ad from looking like it was designed by the same person who did the Tower of Pisa. Flow aids the reader's eye to move in a logical direction through the ad, from one element to the next. The flow can be circular or curved, guiding the reader to the advertiser's name, phone number, or whatever. The average person typically reads from left to right and from top to bottom. The eye will also move naturally from a large element to a smaller one. Many professional artists use a "Z" eye pattern in their layouts. As you can see, visual interest starts at the top left, moves across to top right, then diagonally down to bottom left, finishing up at bottom right. Keep the path of normal eye-flow movement in mind when planning your ad layout, and place the parts of your ad in it in relation to their importance. Layout unity will give the ad a cohesive look rather than the appearance of fragmented elements that seem unrelated.

Offend the reader's eye and he or she will skip over your ad and go on to "Dear Abby" or the comics—and you will have lost a potential customer.

Layouts come in varying degrees of completion.

Thumbnail Layouts: Thumbnail layouts are proportionately small in size and done very quickly. They are the first doodles of the artist, simple in appearance, and containing just enough detail to convey an impression. The experienced artist will usually work up several thumbnail sketches before selecting one to do full size.

Rough Layouts: Rough layouts (or tissues) are done in the actual size of the ad, indicating the major elements and their placement with a small amount of detail (see Figure 4–1). The balance, flow, and unity of the design is established at this point.

Finished Layouts: Finished layouts are completed with enough detail so they can be used for advertiser approval (see Figure 4–2). Illustrations, photos, copy, and lettering are clearly and neatly indicated in their proper size and position.

Comprehensive Layouts: Comprehensive layouts (comps) are taken a step further toward completion and, as a result, are the most

Preliminary Drawing

Rough Layout

Fig. 4–1 Rough layout.

expensive. Headlines, and sometimes the copy, are set in type and pasted in position. Photographs may be taken, not merely indicated. Comp layouts are normally for use when the advertising budget is large enough to justify the high cost of the comp. Small advertisers don't require this form of layout.

fourteen ideas for better layouts

You can do a better job of designing your next ad if you remember these points:

1. Keep your layout simple, particularly when you have many segments to consider. One of advertising's most memorable ads featured a front view, black-and-white photo of a Volkswagen with a two-word headline, "Think Small." Simple, but powerful.

38

Fig. 4–2 Finished layout.

2. Have a strong focal point as your center of attraction, usually your headline or photo. When using a photo, try to incorporate some story appeal—something of interest that will make the reader want to find out what's happening. Crest Toothpaste ran an ad that featured a large photo of a cute baby, smack dab in the middle of the page. The baby's wide open mouth exposed a single, brand new, baby tooth. On one side was the mother proudly pointing to the tooth; and on the other side was dad, smiling in its direction. No matter how hard you tried, you couldn't keep your eyes away from that kid's tooth. A great example of focused attention and arrested eye flow.

3. Use photographs that have interest appeal; they should lure the reader into the ad.

4. Eliminate unnecessary details. Resist the temptation to fill every nook and cranny of white space.

5. Avoid clutter. A messy house is uninviting to enter, and a cluttered ad will turn away the reader. Remember, the more you keep your elements organized and arranged in a logical order, the less confusing the layout will be to your reader. Individually and collectively, they should be pleasing to the eye and inviting to read.

6. Don't get artsy and fill the page with wild decorative devices like rainbows, stars, and explosions. Gus Hartoonian, art director for the *Chicago Tribune*, said that a layout ". . . is not the place to become design crazy. Think of the reader. Don't become gimmick-happy." The reader should not be aware of the ad's design, only the message—always the message.

7. Use lines or shapes that have a tendency to point. For example, a few lines of italic (slanted) type can lead the eye to a photo.

8. Tie several small related pieces together to create the impression of one large unit. A tight group of small photos have more impact together than they do separately.

9. Try using a device that will unify and hold the total ad together, such as a box, border, rule, or white space. If you can't come up with anything better, use a bold border.

10. Keep your copy as long or as short as it takes to say what you need to say, *then stop!*

11. Avoid setting any copy in less than 8-point size type. It's too hard to read. It's better to cut a few words.

12. Don't use too many different type styles in your ad. Roman Mayer, president of Mayer/Martin, Inc., advises, "Use as few typefaces as possible, stay within one type family. It holds your ad together. Ads with too many typefaces can easily get lost, especially if they're placed on a page with many ads."

13. Don't settle for the first layout you come up with. Try several (at least six) approaches. You'll be amazed at how they will improve. Use good, old-fashioned common sense and simple logic for your layout solutions.

14. Once you have developed a layout format that works, carry it through for all of your print advertising. The repeated use will increase recognition of your company and its products.

Don't forget, your reader is an intelligent human being with little time to waste deciphering advertisements. Make your ad attractive and easy to read and you'll be rewarded by having it read. Once read, you have the possibility of a sale.

camera-ready artwork—
putting it all together

It seems that pasting-up artwork is quickly becoming a favorite national pastime. I have seen presidents of large corporations and businesspeople of all walks of life laboriously cutting, snipping, assembling, and gluing pieces of typeset copy and art; struggling to fit them together into some sort of order to create an ad, a mailer, or a folder. And that's okay. On small unimportant jobs, paste-ups can be a do-it-yourself project. But when it comes to artwork that is complex, artwork that is important, artwork that has to reflect the quality of the product it advertises, artwork that will be printed in more than one color, or artwork that will be printed in large quantities, then it's time to hire a commercial artist to do the job. The manner and accuracy in which artwork is prepared has a direct effect on the quality and cost of the final printed piece. Artwork should be done by a professional; a person who doesn't know how to put various art elements together properly can cause the cost of printing to go up, up, and up.

The final assembly of all typeset copy and art elements into one complete piece of artwork is called the "camera-ready artwork," "mechanical," "finished paste-up," "keyline," or, simply, "artwork." I prefer the term "camera-ready artwork"; it's the most descriptive—artwork that is ready for the printer's camera (see Figure 4–3). What are the elements that make up camera-ready artwork? They are, simply, type (the printed message typeset and ready for reproduction), art (photos, drawings, cartoons, etc.) and your signature (logo, company name and address).

Although preparing artwork for reproduction is not as complicated as designing the plans for a three-stage rocket, neither is it as simple as placing art elements, helter-skelter, all over a piece of paper. Doing a piece of professional artwork requires numerous talents: some knowledge of the different printing processes, a certain amount of artistic skills, attention to detail, a degree of patience, and personal neatness.

Let's review the various stages a professional artist goes through in producing artwork; maybe you can pick up some helpful pointers.

Using an approved layout as a guide, the artist begins by measuring the outer area of the layout and outlines it on a piece of heavyweight drawing board, using either a soft #2 black pencil or a nonreproducible light blue pencil. A T-square is used to align all horizontal lines and a triangle for all vertical lines.

When the outline is completed, the artist inks in (with a

41

Fig. 4–3 Camera-ready artwork.

fine-line pen) "crop marks" in the margins, beyond the borders. Crop marks are indications to the printer where the final printed piece is to be trimmed. When artwork or color will extend to the edge of the area to be printed, a one-eighth-inch space (called "bleed") has to be added to allow for minor inaccuracies of printing, folding, or trimming. Fold lines (to show where the piece will fold) are designated by broken lines like this - - - - - - -, so they will not be confused with crop marks by the printer.

The next step is to mark guidelines for use in positioning the different elements to be mounted; usually this is done with the nonreproducible light blue pencil I mentioned previously.

Following the guidelines, the various components—the type, drawings, logos, cartoons, and so on—can then be mounted. Type proofs are trimmed to within one-quarter of an inch from any printed matter. To adhere the elements, the artist can use either rubber cement or

42

mounting wax. When rubber cement is used, the artist coats the back side of each piece and the areas they are to fit into on the board. The cement is allowed to dry, and then each piece is carefully lined up and accurately placed in position; the elements are permanently mounted and cannot be moved. Excess cement is removed from the board with a "pickup" made from dry pieces of rubber cement. When mounting wax is used, only the back of each piece is coated with wax; no wax is placed on the board. When the elements are in position, they are rubbed to create a secure bond. Unlike rubber cement, waxed pieces can easily be lifted and repositioned. (Note: Any artwork mounted with wax should be treated with care and not exposed to the sun or left in a heated area, since the wax will soften, and the elements could possibly shift position.)

Areas where photographs are to appear can either be outlined (keylined) in ink; or they can be blocked in, using a red, adhesive-backed, acetate film. On the printer's negative, the red film will appear as a "window" of clear space that the printer uses to "strip in" (place in position) a photograph. Photos can be mounted directly on the board, like the other components, but first they have to be reduced or enlarged to the actual size in which they will appear. They also have to be properly prescreened (screening is a process for converting a photograph, with all of its tones, into line art).

In preparing artwork for printing in two or more colors, the artist will "overlay" a piece of transparent acetate or velum for each color on the basic board. All elements or areas to appear in color are placed in position on the appropriate overlay sheet. "Register marks" are put on each overlay so they can be accurately aligned.

After the artwork is completed or "pasted-up," it is covered with a "flap" of heavy paper to protect it. The artwork is now ready to be printed in its final form (see Figure 4–4).

Camera-ready artwork—artwork ready for the printer's camera. When it's simple, go ahead and do it yourself. But when it's important to you, hire a professional artist who can put it all together for you.

do-it-yourself artwork—
graphic aids for art, lettering, and line work

If part of all of your advertising is on a do-it-yourself basis because of budget limitations, try some of the easy-to-use graphic aids on the market. This is what advertising agencies, art studios, and large company art departments do, so why not you?

Fig. 4–4 Finished ad.

clip art

Would you believe that a large corporation, with an advertising budget of four million dollars, subscribes to an inexpensive clip-art service? That's like trying to imagine Henry Ford going to Ohrbachs for his clothes. But, illogical as it may seem, many large corporations and many large advertising agencies and art studios do indeed subscribe to some form of clip-art service. They have found that clip art is an effective alternative for those situations and times when custom artwork isn't necessary or financially practical (they want to save money, too).

What is "clip art" (see Figure 4–5)? It's ready-made artwork,

44

Fig. 4–5 Examples of clip-art booklets, which offer a selection of ready-to-use drawings on a broad range of subjects. *Courtesy Volk Clip Art, Pleasantville, NJ 08232.*

in printed form, that usually comes in a booklet and can be cut out (clipped) and reproduced. Normally, it is available on a subscription basis, with a different booklet issued monthly. The typical clip-art booklet contains about a dozen or so different drawings, all with a single theme, that the subscriber can use to his or her heart's content. For example, a "sports" clip-art booklet will feature drawings depicting people participating in baseball, swimming, golf, tennis, or other sporting events. A "holidays" booklet will probably offer a variety of drawings on the Easter bunny, a religious theme, Washington, Lincoln, and something appropriate for St. Paddy's Day, plus an assortment of other holiday-related subjects.

By subscribing to or purchasing clip art, you get nonexclusive rights to reproduce the booklets' contents. You may use all of the artwork as often and as many times as you wish. However, the artwork may not be resyndicated.

Clip art can come in handy when you've reached the end of your deadline rope, and there isn't time left to have original artwork produced.

It's easy to use. You simply select the drawing you want, clip it out of the booklet, and paste it into your advertising message. The professional-caliber artwork is printed in black ink on only one side of a page of reproduction-quality-grade paper for this purpose.

If the drawing is not the right size, your printer can enlarge or reduce it to fit your needs. You can use the complete drawing as is or cut out the portion that meets your requirements.

Clip-art services offer a vast selection of preprinted drawings of men, women, children, animals, and other popular subjects. There are a variety of work and play situations—home, office, travel, stores, and so on—in assorted sizes. Just name a subject from "A" to "Z" and it's probably covered. A few of the categories are "ad-starters," "couples," "family," "medicine," "safety," "tourism," "winter," and "zanies."

Decorative, hand-lettered headlines and complete alphabets reflecting seasonal or holiday themes and attention-getting graphics come in clip-art booklets also.

Some services even provide separated, full-color clip art created by top-notch professional illustrators. Each drawing is color separated, prescreened, and presented as line art. It's an easy and economical way to try full-color art if you have been thinking about it.

The quality is good. The multitude of illustrations, cartoons, stylized drawings, line-converted photographs, graphic elements, and abstract and realistic symbols in many different styles are produced by talented, commercial artists.

The artwork comes in a variety of techniques and artistic

styles—pen and ink, dry brush, litho crayon, pencil, and so on—all of it crisp, clean, and ready for reproduction.

Clip art will reproduce well by any of the popular printing methods—instant printing, photo offset, letterpress, or silk screen.

Clip-art uses are many. You can find representative clip art to liven up and/or improve your company's image. It can be included in your business forms, letterheads, logos, memo pads, invoices, collection notices, and so on. You can use it in newspaper ads, bulletins, company publications, flyers, direct-mail pieces, dealer aids, brochures, booklets, slides, menus, banners, and even television cards. There are clip-art books available that feature decorative borders, ornamentation motifs, fancy rules, frames, and coupons rendered in classic, contemporary, art nouveau, pop, and art deco design styles. It makes it simple to dress up an award certificate, discount coupon, or ad.

Since clip art is not exclusive, it's possible that another advertiser may use the same drawing at the same time and in the same publication you do, but the possibility of this happening is pretty rare.

For more information about clip art services, write to the following:

Volk Clip Art
Box 72
Pleasantville, New Jersey 08232

Dynamic Graphics, Inc.
6707 No. Sheridan Road
Peoria, Illinois 61614

dry-transfer lettering

Up until the fifteenth century, manuscripts, books, and scholarly works were hand-lettered by religious monks, letter by letter, page by page. Each letter had to be slowly and painstakingly drawn by hand. It was demanding work that required the discipline of a West Point cadet, the dedication of a 50-mile marathoner, and the patience of a diamond cutter.

But today, we don't have to letter by hand; we have dry-transfer letters. Dry-transfer (sometimes referred to as "rub down" or "pressure sensitive") letters are individual letters that you quickly and effortlessly rub onto your artwork to form words. The monks would have loved it.

The letters are printed with a special vinyl ink on the underside of a strong, pliable, transparent plastic sheet, approximately 8¼ × 11¼ inches in size. A typical sheet contains a complete alphabet with capital and lower-case letters, numerals, and punctuation marks—all in the same type size and style; extras of the most frequently used letters are included. Each sheet has a removable, protective backing that helps keep the adhesive letters from picking up unwanted lint and dirt.

The letters transfer smoothly and easily to most drawing surfaces, films, vellums, and drafting cloths. Many are heat resistant for diazo copying.

To do transfer lettering, first position the sheet of letters over the art paper or board on which you are working (see Figure 4–6). When the letter you want is in position, determined by the predrawn guideline, you rub it with a soft, blunt tool, such as a commercial burnisher, ballpoint pen, or dull pencil (see Figure 4–7). As you rub the letter, it will transfer and adhere to the surface below. To form a word, you simply repeat the process with each letter; it's that simple. After a word is completed, the protective backing paper is placed over it and rubbed a final time for perfect adhesion (see Figure 4–8). A few brands offer a built-in system of guidelines on the sheets to help you leave the correct amount of space between letters.

If you make a mistake (no one is perfect), corrections can be

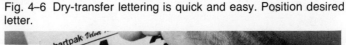

Fig. 4–6 Dry-transfer lettering is quick and easy. Position desired letter.

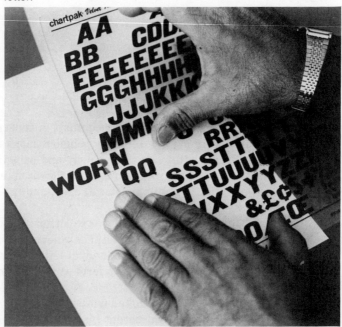

Fig. 4–7 Rub over letter with a burnisher (soft, blunt tool). Remove sheet by carefully lifting from corner.

easily made with a pencil eraser or a commercial pickup, or you can lift off the image with transparent tape.

A quality brand of transfer letters will have such sharp and clean images that they can be enlarged up to 300% and still be satisfactorily reproduced by any popular printing process.

There are over 200 different type styles from which to choose. Sizes range from 8 points (approximately ⅛ inch) to 180 points (approximately 2¼ inches); the larger sized letters (one inch and above) will normally require two or more sheets to complete an alphabet. All alphabets are printed in black, although several are obtainable in white and a few colors.

In addition to letters, you can also get dry-transfer sheets that feature numbers, arrows, or a variety of symbols, such as stars, asterisks, triangles, squares, dots, copyright slugs, brackets, and musical notes. For architectural use, there are sheets of vehicle, furniture, figure, and foliage illustrations. If you want to have your logo (or some other frequently used design) in dry-transfer form, most manufacturers will custom-print sheets for you.

Fig. 4–8 For maximum adhesion, place backing sheet over letter and rub again.

Standard dry-transfer lettering sheets are inexpensive and cost just a few dollars each.

For indoor and outdoor sign use, you can get self-adhesive, plastic (PVC) letters. They come in a wide range of sizes and colors and offer a simple-to-follow spacing system that makes it easy to assemble and align the letters for very professional results. The letters are ideal for marking vehicles, directional signs, doors, exhibition graphics, and all types of displays.

graphic tapes

For the person who can't draw a straight line, there is also help. It's called "graphic tapes" (see Figure 4–9) and they're the answer when you're called upon to produce that straight line.

Graphic tapes are preprinted lines (they also come with designs) that come in roll form, similar to masking tape. They are self-adhesive and easy to apply. To use the tape, first rule in a guideline,

50

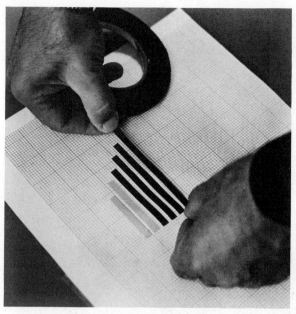

Fig. 4–9 Graphic tapes eliminate hours of repetitive handwork in making charts and graphs.

preferably with a nonreproducible light blue pencil. Next, press a length of the tape in position over the guideline (see Figure 4–10). When you reach the end of the line, you cut off the excess tape and you're done; it's that easy. If you make a mistake or change your mind, the tape can be peeled off and the steps repeated.

Some tapes are flexible enough to form curved and irregularly shaped lines; these are handy for preparing sales charts, maps, printed circuit-board layouts, graphs, and cross-section drawings.

Artists, printers, strippers, and photographers can find special production tapes with Ben Day patterns, solid and broken rules (in a variety of widths), register marks, crop marks, and litho blockout lines (see Figure 4–11). They come in a wide range of sizes, from 1/64-inch to 2 inches wide, patterns and colors, and in both gloss and dull matte finishes.

Graphic tapes can eliminate hours of tedious artwork and can increase the quality of your flip charts, slides, posters, signs, advertisements, house organs, news letters, direct-mail pieces, and the like.

A roll of graphic tape won't cost you much; the cost will vary depending on the pattern and size you select.

Fig. 4–10 Decorative tapes are easy to use. You simply press a length of tape into position and cut off the excess.

time-saving tools

I was talking to a client recently when something I said triggered him to reach into a drawer and pull out an object. Pointing to it, he said, "You know, this is the best damn thing you ever told me about." The object he was referring to was a glue stick. Since he was so impressed with this little time saver, I thought I'd tell you about it and some of the other small but very useful items that advertising people keep in their desk drawers.

A glue stick, as the name implies, is a clear, wax-like glue that comes in a small tube. It's used much like a lipstick, only you apply glue to a piece of paper instead of putting color on lips. It's nontoxic and can't spill or leak. A glue stick is particularly handy when you have to paste up many small pieces of paper. You can also use it to tack the corners of large sheets for quick mounting. It's available in small- and large-size tubes.

If you prefer a liquid adhesive, try Pentel's "Roll 'N Glue." It comes in a bottle that has a roller ball at one end. To apply the glue, you

52

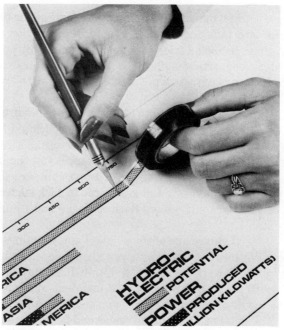

Fig. 4–11 A large variety of easy-to-apply symbols are available for use on artwork, maps, presentations, slides, and so on. *Photo courtesy of Chartpak.*

simply roll it on, similar to the way a roll-on deodorant is applied. Roll 'N Glue dries quickly and is available in regular and extra strengths.

For cutting paper, boards, plastic sheets, and the like, single-edge industrial razor blades are used by most artists in the business. The blades are inexpensive and disposable; you just use one until it doesn't cut well and then throw it away. The blades come individually sheathed in boxes of 100. For delicate work, such as cutting overlay masks and silk-screen stencils, many artists prefer to use "X-Acto" knives. The knife blades are replaceable, come in a variety of point shapes, and are surgically sharp. They come in a set that contains one knife and five assorted blades.

Remember, when handling sharp cutting tools, to be careful, and keep a package of band-aids nearby.

For general-purpose cutting, everyone should have a good pair of scissors. The choice of blade length and handle shape is strictly a case of personal preference; select a pair that fits your hand easily and is comfortable to use. Scissors will last you a long time, so buy a pair of good quality that cut sharply and smoothly.

53

For maneuvering small pieces of paper or objects, "artist's tweezers" are indispensable. If you have ever tried to hold a piece of freshly glued paper or tried to retrieve a small object that fell into your typewriter, you can imagine how useful tweezers can be. You'll find 4¼-inch tweezers with sharp, "pointed" tips or with "round"- or "spade"-shaped tips.

When you have to clean smudges and dirt on your work, use one of the typist's best friends, "Snopake" or "Liquid Paper." Correction fluid is not only good for correcting typing errors, it's great for cleaning up artwork, press releases, photocopy material, and the like. It's a smooth, white, opaque liquid that, when dry, won't chip, crack, or peel. You can even type or mark over it, and it adheres to slick surfaces, such as plastic sheets or photographic paper. Both Snopake and Liquid Paper are inexpensive items.

If you're one of those, like I am, who finds it more difficult to read small letters and numbers, you should consider investing in a magnifying glass. I have a Bausch & Lomb Rectangular Magnifying Glass (#81–33–79) that has a 3⅞-inch × 2-inch lens and a 9-inch focus. It was given to me as a gift, and I first considered it a luxury item, but I was wrong. The glass makes it much easier and faster to retouch fine details in my work and to read small type. It's not a luxury—it's a necessity. Prices for magnifiers will vary, depending on the magnification.

All of us have drawers full of marker pens. Check through your supply and see if you have a Pilot "Fineliner" (#SW–PP) pen marker. It has an extra-hard fine plastic point that retains its shape and enables you to draw light, thin lines. It's ideal for making column rules, borders, or crop marks. The Fineliner comes in a variety of bright, smudge-free colors. For even finer lines, look at the Pilot "Razor Point."

Another good marker is the "Sharpie" (#3000). It's permanent, waterproof, and comes in handy for marking on almost any surface (photographs, plastic overlays, etc.). They are available in fast drying black, red, and blue ink colors.

Speaking of pens, Eberhard Faber has a pen on the market that produces a "nonreproducible" blue line. It's great for writing instructions or putting guidelines on artwork without having them reproduced in the printed piece. It's called the "Copy Not" pen.

For measuring inches, picas, and agate lines, get the C-Thru "Graphic Arts Ruler." It has all three calibrations in one handy ruler. This versatile 18-inch vinyl ruler also has proofreaders' marks, printer's rules (hairline to 12 point), ten different percentage screens (10% to solid), halftone screens, and a simplified copy-casting system with 10-point standard and 10-point elite typewriter copy counters. You get all of this on one ruler.

Having problems making curved lines on maps, graphs, or sales charts? Try a "Flexible Curve Ruler" (yes, there is such a thing). It can be shaped to almost any contour and has a raised edge for inking purposes. The adjustable curve holds its shape and stays firmly in position while you work to give you a smooth, professional-looking curved line every time.

To quickly calculate enlargements (or reductions) of photographs and artwork, use a circular "proportional scale." The scale consists of two laminated vinyl discs that you rotate to determine proportions and size percentages. Instructions are printed on the scale, so you don't have to be a math whiz. Learning how to use one takes only a few minutes, and it's well worth it.

Well, there you have it. A list of inexpensive gadgets you'll find helpful in your advertising work. These, the dry-transfer letters, and the graphic tapes are only some of the time saving graphic aids available to the advertising do-it-yourselfer. Dozens of similar items are available in local art supply stores; look them up in the Yellow Pages under "Artist's Material—Retail." You'll find it worth your while to investigate what they have to offer.

how to "scale" artwork and photos

To determine if a piece of artwork or a photograph will fit a specified area, use the "Diagonal Line Method of Scaling" (see Figure 4–12). Scaling is a simple way to calculate how artwork or photographs will proportionately enlarge or reduce. Here's how it's done. A covering sheet of tracing paper is put over the artwork or photo to be scaled. All lines for the scale should be drawn on the tracing paper; never work on the artwork itself. A line is drawn from one corner of the art area or photograph diagonally to and through the opposite corner. The lines are done lightly so as not to cause any indentation in the art piece beneath. At any point where a horizontal line intersects with a vertical line on the diagonal line, the area outlined will be in exact proportion to the original piece.

If you have many elements that have to be enlarged or reduced—a large number of photographs for a catalog, for example—the diagonal line method may prove to be too slow. There are simple slide rules and proportional discs to calculate proportions more quickly available at local art supply stores. Instructions come with them, and after a little practice, a beginner will find them easy to use.

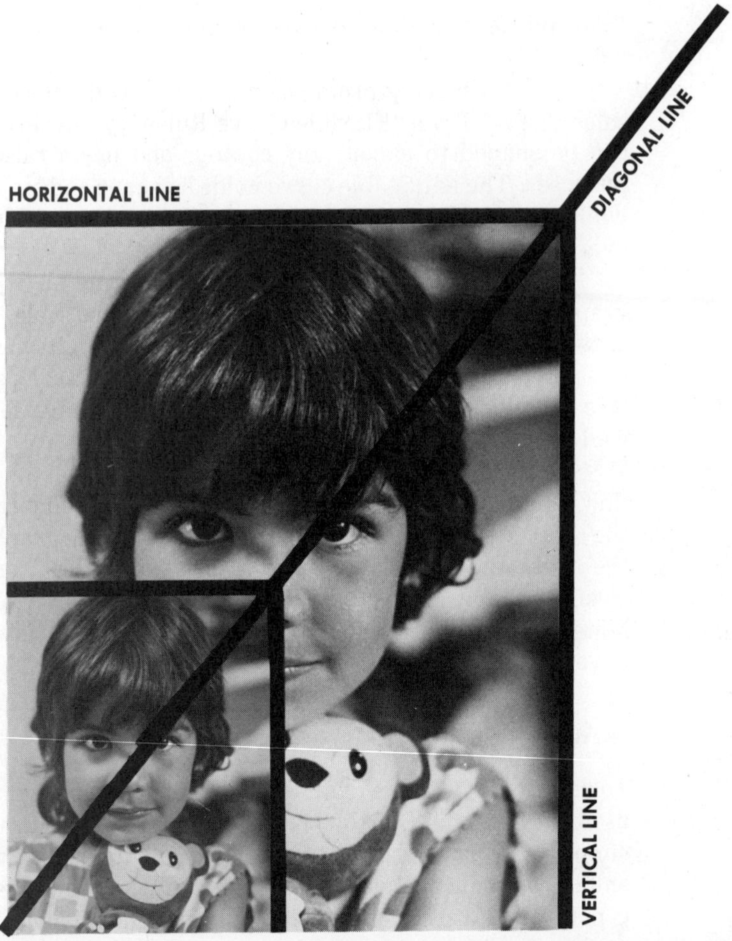

Fig. 4–12 The diagonal line method of scaling for enlarging or reducing artwork or photos. Notice that the diagonal line passes through the same points on both photos.

your company trademark/logo— ways to improve it

Trademarks and logotypes, in one form or another, have been used throughout history. From the beginning of time, craftsmen have developed individual identifying marks and imprinted them on the products they produced. During the medieval period, soldiers were recognized by a distinctive coat of arms emblazoned on their shields and breastplates. They

56

became popular among the aristocrats, who adopted them to distinguish their ancestral heritage. Merchants of the past hung symbolic signs in front of their shops to advertise their wares. Later, in our own country, cattle owners branded livestock with an individual mark to identify their cattle and discourage rustling.

Today, trademarks and logos are used to identify companies and corporations and to single out their products from their competition. In addition to identifying the original manufacturer of a product or service, the device acts as an assurance of quality that a company hopes to project and also serves as a miniature reminder or advertisement for the owner, wherever and whenever it appears.

Although they are used interchangeably, the terms "trademark" and "logotype" actually have different meanings. A trademark is any symbol, name, or graphic design (or combination of these elements) used by a manufacturer to identify a company and its product(s). Sometimes it is called a corporate mark, emblem, insignia, or service mark. The logotype is the name of the sponsor of an advertisement (with or without a trademark) that is usually found at the bottom of an advertisement; it's often referred to as a "logo," "signature," or "sig cut." For our purposes, I'll treat them as one and use the term "trademark/logo."

A trademark/logo can take forms such as the following:

1. Symbols, such as an animal (Borden's Elsie the Cow) or a design that is uniquely shaped (Red Cross). Symbols by themselves are difficult to associate with a product or company unless there is a natural tie-in, such as the camel for Camel cigarettes.

2. Initials, popular with large corporations (IBM, GE, 3M, NBC), need a tremendous amount of exposure before they become well known. Most small companies can't afford the money it takes to achieve identification of an abbreviated name.

3. Names are better to incorporate in a symbol, since there is little doubt as to whom or what the design represents (Coca-Cola, Pan Am, Republic Steel, Xerox).

4. Combining a name with a symbol (Kodak, Kraft, Chevrolet, CBS, General Tire) is one of the more popular forms.

Your company trademark/logo should be original in concept, simple in design, legible, appropriate to the product or service, and easy to remember. For a retailer, it can include one or all of the following elements: (1) store or product name, (2) type of store, (3) address and phone number, (4) a slogan.

Unlike other forms of advertising that have a short lifespan, a trademark/logo is intended to last a long period of time. When choosing a design, it's extremely important to pick one you can live with for many years. Here are some ideas that may help you with your selection:

1. Keep the design clean and simple. It will appear in many forms and sizes during its lifetime, and it should reproduce well in all kinds of media and printing.

2. Include the company address and phone number as an integral part of the artwork, if possible, so this information doesn't have to be set in type each time it appears in print (see Figure 4–13).

3. Avoid lettering that has thin lines. A thoughtfully prepared

Fig. 4–13 With a single, complete modular logo unit, your printer can make up a variety of business forms and stationery.

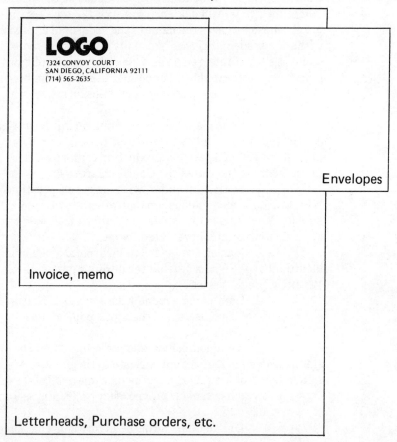

design should be bold enough to reduce to business card size and still be legible. Lines should not break; letters like "a" and "e" should not fill in when they are reduced.

4. Stay away from tints (shades of black or color) in your design. It will continually cost you extra to have the tint properly screened, since paper stocks require different size screens to reproduce them.

5. Slogans are fine, but unless you can really come up with a winner, forget them. Who would believe there is "the bank with a heart?"

6. Don't use exotic typefaces that are popular today but will look outdated in a short time; stay with the classics. For the same reason, avoid people in contemporary fashions, mod hair styles, automobiles or appliances, or similar props. Today's modern car, for example, is tomorrow's antique. Morton Salt and White Rock are two cases of companies that have had to do some updating of their trademark.

Before making a final decision on the selection of a trademark/logo, be absolutely certain you are comfortable with it. In other words, make sure you like it and that it properly reflects your company or product. Don't let the designer impose his or her personal taste on you. You will still be using the concept to represent your company long after the designer has been paid and has departed.

When thinking about developing a new trademark/logo, a good information source is the "General Information Concerning Trademarks" booklet, which is available from the Superintendent of Documents, U.S. Government Printing Office, Washington, D.C. 20402. Have your lawyer make sure no one is using the mark you decide to adopt. It can be done by checking the Principal Register and the Supplemental Register of the U.S. Patent Office. If you want to protect your trademark, have it registered with the U.S. Patent Office, U.S. Department of Commerce, Washington, D.C. 20231, for a period of twenty years (renewable). You should also have it registered with the appropriate agency in your state.

PHOTOGRAPHY

working with professional photographers

Anyone can take professional photographs in 60 seconds with a film-injected Super Duper Instant Camera, right? Wrong! Professional quality photographs are produced by professional photographers using expensive professional equipment.

Television commercials constantly tell us how easy it is for anyone to take pictures; maybe so, but that doesn't mean professional caliber photographs. If you need a picture of food that will make the reader's taste buds jump for joy or a photo of your half-a-mile long factory, you need the talents and skills of a professional photographer.

A professional photographer is expected to be technically proficient in lighting a subject, using the proper film, focusing the camera, and making the proper exposure in order to produce a faithful reproduction of the subject. But that's not enough. A real pro also must have the creative talent and know-how to compose a scene that has eye appeal, drama, and visual impact. He or she must be able to take a simple product, light it, angle it, add a few simple but appropriate props, and create a photo so memorable that consumers will be impressed enough to remember it the next time they are in the supermarket. A real pro can take a city-bred model, put him on a horse, and produce a photograph of a rugged cowboy of the wide open spaces, an image that invites us to identify with him by smoking the same cigarette he does.

Photographers, like other artists, specialize in one or more areas. Their specialties may cover advertising, editorial, magazine, audio-visual, product, or fashion photography. You may find others who limit themselves to architectural, aerial, or underwater photography as well as to formal portraiture and industrial photo-journalism. In small cities, a commercial photographer will usually be a jack-of-all-trades, taking pictures of babies, weddings, school meetings, accidents, news events, and advertising photos of all types.

Photographers charge for their work by the time it takes them to complete an assignment. They will usually quote an hourly fee, a half-day rate, or a rate for a full day's shooting assignment. The costs of film and processing may or may not be included in the rate, depending on the photographer's policy. Outside costs for such things as models and props are always extra. Prices vary from city to city, even from photographer to photographer within the same city; talk to several in your area to get an idea of the prevailing rates.

The fee charged by a photographer does not include rights to the negatives; all negatives remain the property of the photographer. That's right, even though the client pays for them, the photographer owns the negatives; it's an industrywide practice. Your payment covers first rights to the photographs only, unless arrangements are made ahead of time (most photographers will agree to include rights to the negatives for about an additional 50% of the total job price). When a secondary use is necessary, some photographers will expect additional payment.

Before you hire a photographer, it's a good idea to find one who has had some experience in photographing the type of subject you want photographed. You can usually evaluate the photographer's capability by looking at some samples of recent work. Most photographers will be glad to show you a portfolio of their work if you request it.

There are three ways in which you can go about locating a professional photographer:

1. Ask business associates whom they have worked with before and would recommend.

2. Write to the Professional Photographers of America, Inc., a national association. A list of their more than 16,000 members is published annually in the Directory of Qualified Photographic Studios and is available, at no cost, to buyers of photography. The address is Professional Photographers of America, Inc., 1090 Executive Way, Des Plaines, Illinois 60018.

3. Consult the Yellow Pages of the telephone book for photographers in your area. Look under "Photographers—Commercial."

what to do
before the photographer arrives

A few simple precautions can save you both time and money. Before the actual shooting date, the first thing you should do is prepare a list of all subjects to be photographed. Be specific. Include all operations and people. A subject list is very important; it will not only keep you from missing an important shot, but it will also be used by the photographer to accurately evaluate how much time it will take and what kind of equipment will be needed to complete the assignment. The photographer will estimate the cost of the job on the amount of work you want done. Try to get a firm, total-package price that will include all costs for equipment, models (if needed), props, film, processing, prints, and so on. If the assignment is large, avoid hourly rates.

Clean up all areas to be photographed in advance. Remove boxes, wires, and trash from the picture site. Paint machines and equipment when needed.

Make sure all areas and equipment comply with OSHA (Office of Safety and Health Administration) requirements. If there are any negligent areas, you can be sure they will be noticed in the final pictures.

Notify employees, who will appear in the photos, in advance, so they have time to groom themselves; they will appreciate the courtesy.

To have the legal right to publish an individual's photo, you must have written permission. Children under 18 years of age require their parent's or guardian's consent. Every recognizable person in a photo should sign a "model release" form (see Figure 5–1). Model release forms can be supplied by the photographer, or you can purchase a supply at any large photographic supply store. Keep the original signed release form in your files, not in the photographer's; he or she may move or go out of business. Have everyone appearing in your photos sign a release form, even your partner(s). Situations change, and you won't want to be in a position of scrapping an inventory of booklets or an advertisement because some disgruntled ex-employee claimed his or her right to privacy was violated.

Plan ahead. If you feel you will have need for both color and black-and-white photographs, have them taken at the same time; most of the effort in setting up and lighting will have already been done.

Watch your timing. When the outside of your building is to be photographed, study it at different times of the day to determine when the sunlight is most flattering. This simple precaution will avoid scheduling photography when the main part of the building is in deep shadows.

You or your representative should accompany and stay with the photographer while the pictures are being taken to ensure that you get what you need and that everything moves along quickly and smoothly.

Be sure the photographer does as much as possible to avoid costly retouching. It's much easier and less expensive to move a camera a few feet to avoid photographing telephone wires than it is to have a retoucher paint them out in the final print, particularly in color photos.

Simple product shots can be photographed in the photographer's studio. Take time before the shooting session to discuss with the photographer the type of photograph you need and how you plan to use it. The product you supply should be straight off the production line and free from defects and blemishes. If the product is technical in nature, explain as simply as you can how it functions and what its purpose is so the photographer understands the main features of the unit. The photographer will appreciate your presence and help. If you have different opinions as to how a particular photo should be taken, do it both ways. At this stage of the game film is cheap, and you can decide which version to use later, when the

```
+-----------------------------------------------------------+
|                      MODEL RELEASE                        |
|  DATE _____   |
|                                                           |
|  PHOTOGRAPHER _____   |
|                                                           |
|  ADDRESS _____   |
|                                                           |
|  For valuable consideration, I hereby irrevocably consent |
|  to and authorize the use and reproduction by you, or     |
|  anyone authorized by you, of any and all photographs     |
|  which you have this day taken of me, negative or         |
|  positive, proofs of which are hereto attached, for any   |
|  purpose whatsoever, without further compensation to me.  |
|  All negatives and positives, together with the prints    |
|  shall constitute your property, solely and completely.   |
|                                                           |
|  I am over 18 years of age.   YES _____   NO _____      |
|                                                           |
|  MODEL _____   |
|                    Signature of Model                     |
|                                                           |
|  Address: _____   |
|                                                           |
|  Witnessed by: _____   |
|                    Signature of Witness                   |
|                                                           |
|  (If the person signing is under 18 consent should be     |
|  given by parent or guardian, as follows:                 |
|                                                           |
|  I hereby certify that I am the parent or guardian of ___ |
|  _____  |
|  The model named above, and for value received I do give  |
|  my consent without reservations to the foregoing on      |
|  behalf of him or her or them..                           |
|                                                           |
|  DATED _____   |
|                Signature of Parent or Guardian            |
|                                                           |
|  WITNESSED by: _____   |
|                    Signature of Witness                   |
+-----------------------------------------------------------+
```

Fig. 5–1 Example of a typical model release form, which should be signed by every recognizable person appearing in your photos. Standard forms are available in most photographic supply stores.

64

prints are made. Work together as a team for the common good—a better photo for you.

Once a shooting schedule is completed, the photographer will have the exposed film processed and supply you with a set of contact prints (proofs). These are made directly from negatives without enlargement. The photographer will make enlargement prints of the ones you select from the proofs. Expect to pay extra for the prints. Standard enlargement print size is 8×10 inches; other sizes are 4×5, 5×7, 11×14, and 16×20 inches. When ordering prints, ask for the "full negative image" to be printed. Retaining the full image allows you more flexibility in the use of the photo. You can also ask to have the photo "flopped," (see Figure 5–2), which is a reverse image—everything facing left will appear facing right and vice versa. Be careful when you do this since some details, such as signs, will be noticeably wrong.

For advertising purposes, glossy prints rather than matte (rough-surfaced) prints are almost always used; the slick surface adds to the contrast and is better for reproduction.

Maintain a good filing system for your photographs; keep track of where they are sent and when they are returned. If you lose a photo, you will have to go back to the photographer for another print (an extra cost). And if he or she has gone out of business, you'll have to start all over again. Give your ulcer a break and hang onto your photos.

thoughts about using photos

One picture is worth more than ten thousand words.

OLD CHINESE PROVERB

The honorable, gentle person who coined this wise saying might well have been thinking about advertising photographs when he did so. One good photo can, indeed, create a mood, evoke an emotion, or establish a situation that would take reams of written copy to equal. In advertising, the right photograph can convey your message so powerfully and clearly that words and space can be kept to a minimum.

A photograph's greatest asset is its realistic portrayal of people and events. It can clearly show the detail in fine fabric, the rich grain of wood, the frost on a cold glass of beer, or the heart-tugging tear in an eye—all in a way that few drawings can duplicate.

When you use a photograph, be sure you show situations that are natural and believable. If you create a false impression in your photo, your entire ad is subconsciously suspect to the reader.

Fig. 5–2 Flopping a photo.

Sexy photos can sell sexy products, but they seldom sell refrigerators, television sets, appliances, and the like. With hard products, you're better off showing the particular feature that makes your product superior to others. Before-and-after photo demonstrations are an impressive way to emphasize your product's unique advantage. For instance, a before-photo of a microwave oven (with a clock in the background) set to start cooking, alongside an after-photo of the same oven finished cooking, can clearly demonstrate the product's quick cooking capability. A word of advice, don't fake demonstration photos, or you'll have the consumer protection advocates knocking on your door.

Always include a descriptive caption under your photos, especially in product shots. Readership studies indicate photo captions in advertisements are read twice as much as the body copy.

Today's woman is very sensitive to how she is portrayed. Stereotypes of women as sex symbols or housewife drudges can turn her off and earn you a flow of bitter mail from women's groups. If you are in doubt as to how they want to be depicted, ask a few women for their opinions. You'll probably be surprised.

Eliminate detail that doesn't contribute to the ad's message. If you are selling swimsuits and have a photo of a model wearing the suit at the beach, you can take out all of the background. By eliminating the background, you focus on the style and design of the swimsuit without distracting the reader with unnecessary details.

Removing unwanted portions of a photo is called "cropping" and is easily accomplished by putting crop marks in the outside margins of a photo to indicate which portions are to be left out (see Figure 5–3). When indicating crop marks, don't mark directly on the photo itself and never, never cut a photo with scissors; it ruins the photo for possible future use and serves no practical purpose.

When cropping photos, avoid visually amputating people. If you sever a person's photo at a bodily joint, such as the neck, elbow, wrist or ankle, the reader will feel uncomfortable. When you crop near a body joint, always include a small amount of the area from either side of the joint. Crop people at the rib cage when possible; it rids a man of a pot belly and leaves a woman endowed.

Flop your photo if the image is facing the wrong direction. The negative is printed from the opposite side, and the image is reversed. As I mentioned before, watch out when you do this, since lettering will appear backwards, right-handed people will become left-handed, coat jackets will button on the wrong side, and so on. When should you consider flopping a photo? A good time is when the original photo shows a person

$2''$

Fig. 5–3 How to crop a photo.

facing out of an ad; by reversing the image, the person is faced into the advertising message. But remember, be careful.

Avoid imprinting small-size type over a photo. Large, bold headlines can hold up well, but small type becomes difficult to read, particularly on a color photo where color registration is a problem.

People like to see photographs of other people. In your photos, capture that quality of human interest and warmth that can emotionally involve the reader and make him or her want to stop and read the entire ad.

One ad that is read is worth ten thousand ads that go unnoticed—new American proverb.

saving with stock photos

What do you do when you need a photograph of beautiful Mount Fujiyama? Do you pick up the tab to send a photographer packing on an all-expense-paid trip to Japan to capture the majestic beauty of the world-famous mountain? Or suppose you needed a photograph of a marching band parading down a street before a cheering crowd? Do you locate and hire an entire band complete with 76 trombones plus a throng of extras; and when you pay the bill, do you find the accompanying costs similar to those of a small Hollywood production? Or what if you had to have a photo of a hospital surgical operating team? Do you have to pay for the talents of models posing as doctors and nurses, not to mention the patient who will get paid for doing nothing more than lying still? Do you have to foot the bill to rent a surgical room, complete with oxygen tanks, lights, and sophisticated electronic medical monitoring equipment?

Well, you could, but when you don't have the time or budget for such undertakings, why not do what advertising agencies, art studios, and publications do. You can relax in the comfort and sanity of your office, flip through the pages of a "stock photo" catalog (see Figure 5–4), select a photo that meets your needs, and order it by mail.

Stock photos are ready-for-use, specially posed photographs that cover a wide variety of popular situations. Photographs featuring all types of people, places, and activities are available for your use. Scenes of people—young, old, male, female, of all ethnic groups. Interior views—business office, home, church, and so on. Activities—traveling by car, plane, train, boat, or camper; working, vacationing, swimming, golfing, hiking. Near and far away places—Washington, D.C., Hawaii, Egypt; ocean, mountains, or desert.

The catalogs actually show only a small cross-section of the

QF-5005-Z   QA-1915-Z   QR-4846-Z

QP-1777-Z   QG-2074-Z   QS-4787-Z

QJ-2198-Z   QT-808-Z   QC-3427-Z

Fig. 5–4 Typical samples of photos available from a stock photo company.
Courtesy Harold M. Lambert Studios, Philadelphia, PA.

photographs that are available. Stock photo companies have vast collections of photos on file. If you don't see what you want in the firm's catalog, you can write or call them and describe, in detail, the type of photograph for which you are looking. They will be glad to send you several possibilities on an "approval" basis for you to consider. Most companies do not charge for this service; all they require is that you return the unused material to them, usually within ten days, in its original condition. A few companies charge a minimum service fee to cover the cost of processing a request, which is deductible from the reproduction fee if you decide to use one or more of the photos.

When ordering a stock photo, you should be prepared to explain how you intend to use it so a rate for its use can be established. Rates vary according to the manner and extent of a photo's use. The rate for advertising use is determined by the medium, size of space, circulation, and frequency of use. For example, an advertiser planning to use a stock photo in a magazine with low circulation would pay a lower rate than that charged another advertiser for using the same photo in a large circulation magazine. If the photo is to be used editorially, the fee would generally be lower than the advertising-use fee.

Payment of the fee gives you the right to publish the photo for the specified purpose. It also includes legal advertising releases covering recognizable people, individually and in most groups. However, you don't get exclusive rights to the photo. It is conceivable that another advertiser may use the identical photo in the same publication and at the same time you do, but the chance of this happening is pretty rare.

For reproduction purposes, the stock photo company will send you professional quality 8×10 inch glossy black-and-white photographs. For color, 4×5 inch transparencies are supplied, which must be returned after you have used them.

So the next time you have need for a complex photo, such as a doctor performing an operation on the top of Mount Fujiyama to the accompaniment of a marching band, take the easy way out and order a stock photo.

For more information or a stock photo catalog, write to one of the following:

Photofile Ltd.
76 Madison Avenue
New York, New York 10016

Harold M. Lambert Studios
P. O. Box 27310
Philadelphia, Pennsylvania 19150

H. Armstrong Roberts
4203 Locust Street
Philadelphia, Pennsylvania 19104

PRODUCTION

reproducing your advertisement

You have pleaded with, threatened, and cajoled the copywriter to come up with just the right words for your advertisement. You nearly lost your sanity working with an artist from the first layout to the completed artwork. Finally, it's finished and ready to go. Well, almost. There is still one more vital stage to go through before the ad is published. The artwork has to be converted into a form suitable for reproduction. It's called the "production" stage.

Ad production is a complicated process. Even the pros in the business don't know it all: They specialize. However, you should learn as much as you possibly can about how it works. If you know what you can or cannot do or change, you'll be able to avoid extra costs.

In print media, there are three basic forms of reproduction: letterpress, gravure, and offset. The following gives you a brief description of the three different methods.

Letterpress: In this process, the material to be printed is raised from the surface of a metal plate (also called an engraving). It's like using a rubber stamp. The plate is metal, usually made of zinc or copper.

Gravure (or intaglio): This method of printing also employs metal plates, but the image to be reproduced is below the surface of the plate. The image is transferred to the paper by absorption, somewhat like a blotter picks up an inked image.

Offset (lithography): This name is derived from the indirect method used in picking up the image. It uses a flat plate and is based on the principle that grease and water do not mix. The plate does not actually come in contact with the paper; it prints on a roller (called a blanket) that offsets the inked image to the paper. The use of offset lithography by publications has grown rapidly over the past few years because it offers good quality reproduction at a lower cost than the other methods.

The method by which a publication is printed can be found in the mechanical requirements part of its rate card, or in *Standard Rate & Data*, a monthly media information publication available by subscription or in the business reference section of most large libraries.

Also, the method of printing a publication uses determines the form your artwork has to be converted to in order to reproduce properly. If the publication is printed by letterpress, you will have to supply a metal engraving; if it's offset or gravure, you will probably be required to send a duplicate photographic print, stat, or negative of the artwork. These can usually be made by local printers, typesetters, or graphic production companies.

If you can't get the required material produced locally, most publications will be glad to do it for you (at an additional charge) if you send your original artwork. In most cases, however, it's not a good idea to send the original artwork for two obvious reasons: (1) The artwork runs the risk of being lost or damaged (it does happen), and you'd have to go back to square one and start all over again. (2) Your art is tied up should you decide to run the same ad in different publications at the same time or have it printed for use as a mailing piece.

There are several ways to save money when it comes to ad production. Here are a few things to remember:

1. Get an estimate—ask what is needed to be done and how much it will cost. Have it explained to you in simple, nontechnical terms. Don't approve anything you don't understand.

2. Avoid making changes unless it is absolutely necessary. Although minor changes can be made at the production stage, extra costs escalate rapidly.

3. When an ad is scheduled to appear in several different publications, plan to have the artwork prepared so that one size will fit all of them; it will save the expense of additional artwork.

4. Color reproduction is expensive and complicated. Be sure the person handling it for you is experienced—it's not the time to use a beginner. A knowledge of the four-color process is essential, or your costs can go through the ceiling.

5. Request the return of all printing material for which you paid. Most publications and printers destroy engravings, negatives, and so on after a year as a matter of policy, unless otherwise advised by the advertiser.

One of the best ways to learn about production is to actually see how it's done. Ask your newspaper or printing sales representative to give you a personally guided tour of their facilities. They will be flattered you asked and might even spring for lunch. One trip through a printing plant will be more informative than reading a dozen books on the subject.

a simple guide to offset printing

The father of present-day forms of lithography was a Bavarian actor/writer named Alois Senefelder. In 1798, almost by accident, he discovered that the basic chemical principle, "grease and water do not mix," could be used in printing from a flat surface (planography). Today, more than half of our daily newspapers and most of our magazines are printed by photo-offset lithography (more commonly known as offset) on large presses with spinning cylinders carrying water, ink, and paper with a capability of 10,000 to 12,000 printing impressions an hour. Even more efficient are Web offset presses, which can reach speeds of 2,000 feet per minute. Pretty fast, when you consider Senefelder had to do his printing by hand, one sheet at a time.

Let's take a look at how it's done.

Assume you have taken camera-ready artwork for a mailer, or whatever, to an offset printer to be printed. Here's what takes place after you have left.

The printer takes your camera-ready artwork, puts it into a large glass frame, and photographs it, producing a film negative copy (everything white in the original artwork appears black, and all black lines and areas appear white—actually transparent, since you can see through the film). At the same time, any additional art pieces, such as illustrations, hand lettering, or photos, would also be photographed. All the film elements would then be "stripped" (put together, in position) on a ruled sheet called a "flat." Any imperfections, spots, dirt marks, fingerprints, smudges, and the like are "opaqued" (painted) out, so they don't show up later in the printed piece. The flat is then photographically contact printed directly onto a piece of photographic paper. The paper copy print is called a "blueline" because the image appears blue (some paper prints appear in brown and are obviously called "brownlines"). The blueline is a final proof to show a client how the job will appear, with all elements in their proper size and position, before the printing plate is made. Changes after a blueline is made should be avoided, since the production involved in making corrections is costly. However, if a very important change, such as a new address, phone number, or price, has to be made, it can be done.

After the blueline has been approved, the printer then prepares the printing plate. This plate is a thin, flexible sheet of zinc or aluminum that has been grained (roughened) to retain dampness and coated with a light-sensitive emulsion. The image to be printed is photographically transferred from the negative flat to the printing plate itself.

The negative flat is positioned over the plate, and both are put in a glass vacuum frame to be contact printed. A bright arc-light is turned on, and the light passes through the transparent image areas of the negative and hardens the plate's sensitized emulsion coating underneath.

The plate is removed from the frame, thoroughly rubbed overall with a greasy developing ink, and then washed with water. The unhardened portions of the emulsion, which are the blank areas of the artwork, wash away, carrying their coat of ink. But the hardened portions, which represent the areas to be printed, cling to the grained metal, holding the hardened ink in place. The plate is permanently fixed and then cleaned. It's ready for printing.

The flexible printing plate is wrapped and fastened around a metal cylinder on the printing press. Ink, which is greasy in content, is spread uniformly over the press's ink rollers. When the printing press is started, water is introduced, which adheres only to those portions of the plate that do not bear any printing surface. The rotating plate comes in contact with the inking roller with its greasy ink. The ink adheres only to those portions of the plate that contain the image to be printed; other nonprinting areas repel the ink because of their water coating (grease and water don't mix—remember our friend Senefelder).

The freshly inked plate next comes in contact with another cylinder, which is covered with a neoprene material, called a "blanket." The inked image is transferred from the plate onto the blanket and then transferred again, or "offset," (this is where the name offset lithography comes from) onto paper. Notice, the printing plate does not actually come in contact with the paper; the image is printed by the blanket.

The resiliency of the blanket makes it possible to obtain finer detail in illustrations and photographs on soft-textured paper. Offsetting the image on paper via the blanket also reduces the amount of time ordinarily needed when a hard-surfaced metal plate is used in making the press ready (make-ready) for printing.

Very simply stated, that's how your camera-ready artwork is printed by the offset lithographic method. Most printers will be glad to help you in the production of your job for printing and will offer useful suggestions on selecting the appropriate printing papers and ink colors.

different types of printers

Printers, generally, fit into one of three basic types:

1. *Job Printers*—usually small store-front, neighborhood firms specializing in short-run (small quantity) jobs, such as wedding announcements, stationery, business cards, and simple business forms.

2. *Commercial Printers*—specializing in business stationery, business forms of all types, and some advertising literature in color.

3. *Large Commercial Printers*—employing many people and maintaining a large variety of plate-making and printing equipment capa-

ble of producing large runs of publications, booklets, brochures, displays, mailers, and the like in one or multiple colors. In addition to printing, they are capable of folding, binding, embossing, and die-cutting the printed pieces.

There are several things you can do to help keep your printing costs down; here are a few points to keep in mind:

1. Submit clean, professionally prepared, complete, camera-ready artwork whenever possible. The less your printer has to do, the less you will be charged.
2. Don't insist on using an exotic grade of printing paper when a suitable, less expensive paper will do. Special papers have to be ordered in minimum quantities and can increase overall job costs.
3. Don't make unnecessary changes in copy, artwork, or color after you have submitted artwork to the printer. It's all extra work, and you will be billed accordingly.
4. Finally, and most importantly, plan ahead so you don't have to ask the printer to rush. Rush jobs can go into overtime, and you know how expensive that can get.

low-cost, fast, instant printing

During the early 1960's, a special camera was developed that, in one step, could produce a printing plate made of paper. This unique method eliminated much of the time and expense of producing a lithographic negative or metal plate. It made it possible for a new breed of printer to offer customers printing "While-U-Wait." Instant printing was born and spread across the country like a chain of fast-food hamburger stands. Today, small store-front Instant Print shops can be found in almost every city.

Instant printing has become popular with both small and large advertisers alike because it enables them to have mailers, flyers, price lists, letterheads, envelopes, sales letters, catalog sheets, and a variety of other literature printed quickly and inexpensively in minimum quantities.

In addition to providing fast, low-cost printing, some shops also offer services such as 3-hole punching, gluing and padding sheets (memo pads), collating (arranging multiple sheets in proper sequence), and printing in one color other than black.

There are, however, a few limitations to instant printing:

1. Black ink is the only color normally available.
2. Selection of paper is usually limited to what the printer has on hand for same-day service.
3. Sheet size is restricted to 8½ × 11 inches (typewriter page size), 8½ × 14 inches (legal page size) and 17 × 11 inches (which folds to four pages, 8½ × 11 inches).
4. Reproduction quality of instant printing is not as delicate as other, more expensive methods of printing.

When care is taken in preparing the camera-ready artwork prior to printing, satisfactory results can be obtained. Camera-ready artwork is the finished paste-up of art and copy for reproduction. The way in which this paste-up is prepared has a direct effect on the quality of the finished piece.

Remember these few easy-to-follow suggestions, and you can improve the quality of your next instant print job:

1. Before you even start a new job, look through your files for existing artwork to see if anything can be adapted for reuse. Previously used artwork, photographs, and type proofs can sometimes be recycled.

2. Have drawings, diagrams, hand lettering, map locations, and the like made with black India ink or a black fineline felt-tip pen; pencil and ball point lines do not, as a rule, reproduce well.

3. Paste all of your elements on plain white paper—never on colored paper. If you can't get hold of some artist's drawing board, try heavyweight typewriter bond paper; the 8½ × 11 inch size is just right to fit most needs.

4. Use a sharply pointed, nonreproducible, light blue pencil to indicate guidelines and to block in areas. Since the color (light blue) does not reproduce, the lines need not be erased.

5. Keep all artwork and written material ¼-inch away from the edge of the paper. This margin serves as a "gripper" edge for the printing press to hold the paper while it is being printed.

6. Unless you are a professional letterer, don't hand-letter your headlines or bold words. Sloppy hand-lettering doesn't convey an image of quality. Use dry-transfer letters or have the words set in type by a commercial typesetter.

7. For low-budget jobs, you can type most of your copy with an electric typewriter equipped with a black carbon ribbon; manual type-writers do not produce a good, clear image. Be sure to clean the typewriter keys before you start. Typewritten errors can be corrected easily with

either white correction fluid or correction paper. You can also correct errors by retyping the correction on a separate piece of paper and pasting it over the incorrect version. Type the whole paragraph rather than a single word or line. You can be sure your corrections are straight by holding the material up to a light or window and aligning the words.

8. Avoid using photos that have previously been printed in a newspaper or magazine; they will fill in the dark areas and lose much of their detail. To reproduce a photo properly, you have to start with the original and have it prescreened (screening is a process for converting a photograph, with all of its tones, into line copy). The tones are maintained by a halftone screen that converts the photo's varying shades of gray into a series of dots. Your printer can tell you where to have your photo screened. Black-and-white photos reproduce best; but color photos can be printed in black and white, with some loss in quality.

9. Align the various components with an artist's T-square and triangle. A T-square will help keep the elements horizontally straight, and the triangle will aid in aligning vertical units. Check to make sure all lines are straight and square with the page.

10. Limit the amount of both heavy, solid black and reverse (white letters on black) areas. Large areas of black ink are slow in drying and have a tendency to offset on the backs of other sheets during the printing process.

11. Use rubber cement to do your paste-up. For small jobs, you can use a wax or glue stick. Cellophane tape may be used also, but care has to be taken to keep the tape clean. Paste-up marks can appear on the printed piece, so be careful when using any of these methods. Don't forget—be clean and neat at all times!

12. After you have finished, carefully look over your paste-up. Eliminate all lines you don't want to appear in the printed piece. If you can't erase a line or area, paint over it with white, water-soluble poster paint. Clean every fingerprint, smudge, and spot, or the camera will record it.

13. Protect your finished artwork with a flap of covering paper. Don't fold or bend the artwork; you'll run the risk of having a crease mark show up in the printed work.

You can find most of the equipment you will need—black India ink, pens, paper, blue pencils, dry-transfer letters, rubber cement, glue sticks, T-squares, triangles, white poster paint, and so on—at your local art supply store.

When your artwork is finished, you're ready to head to your

local instant print shop. If you don't know of one in your area, check the Yellow Pages under "Printers."

the halftone screen—understanding how a photograph is reproduced

Many an advertising do-it-yourselfer has, at one time or another, taken a piece of artwork he or she has lovingly created to an instant printing shop only to be told the piece couldn't be printed—"because it had a photograph in it."

If you've had this problem but never had it clearly explained to you, stay with me a few minutes, and I'll give you a brief rundown.

For starters, if a black-and-white photo were to be reproduced "as is," the result would be a stark, poster-like effect; everything darker than middle gray would appear solid black, and everything lighter than middle gray would be pure white. The middle values of gray in the photo would be completely lost.

As I've mentioned before, the method of reproducing a photograph is known as the halftone screen process. This process preserves the photo's appearance, with all of its various shades of gray, by converting the image into thousands of tiny dots. The reader's eye blends these dots into smooth areas of gray tone.

The procedure is fairly simple. The original continuous tone photo is rephotographed through a halftone screen. The screen is made of two pieces of clear plastic, each ruled with fine parallel lines. The pieces are bonded together with the lines, at right angles to each other. The result is a mesh screen with literally thousands of small windows (openings) in it. Imagine looking at a photograph through a window screen and you'll get the effect.

The many openings in the screen are of equal size, but the dots must be of varying sizes so the reader's eye will be able to blend them into the shades of gray being duplicated. Take a magnifying glass and look at a photograph in any newspaper or magazine, and you will be able to see the individual pattern of dots to which I'm referring. You'll find the dots are large and close together where the photo is dark; but where it is light, the dots are much finer and seemingly farther apart. Actually, the center of the dots are equi-distant from each other; the dots vary in size only. To accomplish this pattern of dots, the screen is positioned a minute distance from the film surface. This allows the light to spread as it passes through each hole in the screen, producing dots of different sizes, depending on the shade of gray. All of the dots are solid black—it's the reader's eye that blends the black dots with the white of the paper to see a gray tone.

After the image of the photograph has passed through the screen, it transfers onto a piece of sensitized film, similar to the film you use to take black-and-white snapshots with, and a negative image is formed. This negative is contact-printed directly onto photographic paper in positive form; this screened print is called a "velox." If an engraving is needed, a piece of sensitized metal is used instead of the film; it is referred to as a "halftone," "zinc," "plate," "cut," or "engraving." They all define the same thing—a metal copy of the photo.

Halftone screens come with different line rulings (see Figure 6–1), ranging from "coarse" screens with as few as 50 lines per lineal inch to very "fine" screens that have up to 300 lines. The most used are 65- (see Figure 6–2), 85- (see Figure 6–3), 110- (see Figure 6–4), 120-, 133- (see Figure 6–5), and 150-line screens. A 110-halftone screen would have 110 lines to the lineal inch. A square inch would then have 110×110, for a total of 12,100 openings. It is referred to as a "110-screen" or a "110-line screen"; both mean the same thing—110 dots to the lineal inch.

Most newspapers require a photo to be either a 65- or 85-screen. When a finer screen is used on newsprint, the dots tend to fill in, and the photo appears blurred and smudged. In addition, any detail in the photo is usually lost. For best results in newspapers, use a photo with good contrast—strong black-and-white areas.

The majority of magazines and trade journals specify 110- or 120-screen for their grade of paper. Photos that have a good middle-value tonal range reproduce best here.

Most commercial offset printers have a variety of halftone screens and can print photographs on all grades of paper. However, the smaller, instant print shops do not have this capability and require a photo be prescreened (65- or 85-line) before they can print it. You can usually have this done by an engraver or typesetting company.

If your next job contains a photo and is destined for your favorite instant printer, be prepared. Include a screened print with your material, and you'll save yourself a lot of time and trouble.

tips on typography

Have you ever seen an ad that resembled an eye chart in an optometrist's office? The sentences were so cut up they didn't make sense, or the words were so small you needed a magnifying glass to read the fine print. Or how about an ad that looked like a hand grenade exploded in the middle of it,

Fig. 6–1

scattering the message all over the page at crazy angles? These kinds of advertisements suffer from typographic pollution—even worse, they don't get read.

In *Publishers' Auxiliary*, Dr. Earl Newsom noted, "Material they [the readers] often bypass as hard to read includes that set in too small a type size, in too long a line or a combination of the two without adequate leading (spacing)."

An advertisement should be inviting to look at and easy to read. It's that simple. The appearance of an ad can be enhanced by knowing just a little bit about typography. Type is quite versatile. It can be used to

82

Fig. 6–2

Fig. 6–3

Fig. 6–1 Section of a screened photo enlarged. Note that all dots are black: Your eye blends the white of the paper with the various sized dots to create the tones of gray.

Fig. 6–2 65-halftone screen, used for coarse grade reproduction. Note that individual dots are visible to your naked eye.

Fig. 6–3 85-halftone screen, used by most newspapers and for instant printing.

Fig. 6–4 110-halftone screen, used for average magazine reproduction.

Fig. 6–5 133-halftone screen, for quality reproduction. Notice that although you are unable to see any dots, they are there.

Fig. 6–4

Fig. 6–5

suggest a desired effect, such as masculinity, femininity, strength, formality, delicacy, and so on; it all depends on how it's used.

In selecting type, two factors have to be considered—readability and legibility. Readability is the ease with which a printed page can be read. It is influenced by the style and size of the type and the spacing between words, letters, and lines. Legibility refers to the speed with which each letter or word can be recognized by the reader, and it is affected by the design of the typeface.

A type*face* (also called a *font)* is a single design of type containing all the letters of the alphabet, numerals, and punctuation marks. Some faces also vary in weight and shape within a single style—light, medium, bold, extra bold, expanded, or condensed (see Figure 6–6).

Recognizing the many different styles is a problem, since many type styles are similar in appearance; even the pros have a difficult time telling some of them apart. For the beginner, the following classifications of type are an easy way to become familiar with the basic characteristics (see Figure 6–7).

Roman Typefaces: Roman type is identified by thick and thin strokes in the letters, with serifs (short horizontal lines) at the top and bottom of most of the letters. Roman-style typefaces are used by many newspapers and magazines because they are considered highly readable.

Gothic Typefaces: Gothic type (also called "sans serif") can be recognized by the uniform thickness of the lines; the letters *do not have serifs*. Its simple, clean appearance makes it a popular style among designers.

Square Serif Typefaces: In square serif type, the letters are generally uniform in thickness and *have* square or blocked serifs. This face is used mostly for headlines and small amounts of copy matter.

Script and Text Typefaces: Script and text types are designed to imitate handwriting and old-style hand-lettering. They are limited in use to formal announcements and invitations. It's difficult to read large amounts of copy in script faces—use it sparingly.

Miscellaneous Typefaces: The many decorative type styles on the market are so unique they defy classification. If you run across a type style that doesn't seem to fit into any of the above categories, just consider it miscellaneous.

points and picas— the basic units of measure

The "point" and the "pica" are two units of measure universally used in the typesetting and printing industries.

A Frenchman, Pierre Simon Fournier (1712–1768) is credited with being the founder of the point system, which makes it possible to measure type with greater precision than the standard inch method. Points are used to measure and express the size (height) of typeset letters (10 point Helvetica, 12 point Caslon, etc.). A single point measures $1/72$

VEGA LIGHT, SMALL CAPS, AND ITALIC

ABCDEFGHIJKLMNOPQRSTUVWXYZ&
⅛ ¼ ⅜ ½ ⅝ ¾ ⅞ ⅓ ⅔
abcdefghijklmnopqrstuvwxyz ff fi fl ffi ffl
1234567890$¢.,-;'"?!()——*%
ABCDEFGHIJKLMNOPQRSTUVWXYZ
1234567890$ []¿¡/···· ^^~``,
+ × = ÷ ' ' ° • |_ #

ABCDEFGHIJKLMNOPQRSTUVWXYZ&
abcdefghijklmnopqrstuvwxyz ff fi fl ffi ffl
1234567890$.,-;'?!()¿¡

The purpose of good typography is to present the
message clearly and legibly for fast, easy reading
and comprehension. It should also impart a smart,
well-groomed look that adds both appearance and
appeal. A careful analysis of the purpose for which
the printed piece is intended will aid the selection

VEGA, SMALL CAPS, AND ITALIC

ABCDEFGHIJKLMNOPQRSTUVWXYZ&
⅛ ¼ ⅜ ½ ⅝ ¾ ⅞ ⅓ ⅔
abcdefghijklmnopqrstuvwxyz ff fi fl ffi ffl
1234567890$¢.,-;'"?!()——*%
ABCDEFGHIJKLMNOPQRSTUVWXYZ
1234567890$ []¿¡/···· ^^~``,
+ × = ÷ ' ' ° • |_ #

ABCDEFGHIJKLMNOPQRSTUVWXYZ&
abcdefghijklmnopqrstuvwxyz ff fi fl ffi ffl
1234567890$.,-;'?!()¿¡

The purpose of good typography is to present
the message clearly and legibly for fast, easy
reading and comprehension. It should also impart a smart, well-groomed look that adds both
appearance and appeal. A careful analysis of
the purpose for which the printed piece is in-

VEGA MEDIUM, SMALL CAPS, AND ITALIC

ABCDEFGHIJKLMNOPQRSTUVWXYZ&
⅛ ¼ ⅜ ½ ⅝ ¾ ⅞ ⅓ ⅔ + × = ÷ ' ° • |_ #
abcdefghijklmnopqrstuvwxyz ff fi fl ffi ffl
1234567890$¢.,-;'"?!()——*%
ABCDEFGHIJKLMNOPQRSTUVWXYZ
1234567890$ []¿¡/···· ^^~``,

ABCDEFGHIJKLMNOPQRSTUVWXYZ&
abcdefghijklmnopqrstuvwxyz ff fi fl ffi ffl
1234567890$.,-;'"?!()¿¡

**The purpose of good typography is to present
the message clearly and legibly for fast, easy
reading and comprehension. It should also impart a smart, well-groomed look that adds both
appearance and appeal. A careful analysis of
the purpose for which the printed piece is in-**

VEGA BOLD, SMALL CAPS, AND ITALIC

ABCDEFGHIJKLMNOPQRSTUVWX
YZ& ⅛ ¼ ⅜ ½ ⅝ ¾ ⅞ ⅓ ⅔ ff fi fl ffi ffl
abcdefghijklmnopqrstuvwxyz
1234567890$¢.,-;'"?!()——*%
ABCDEFGHIJKLMNOPQRSTUVWXYZ
1234567890$ []¿¡/···· ^^~``,
+ × = ÷ ' ° • |_ #

ABCDEFGHIJKLMNOPQRSTUVWX
YZ& abcdefghijklmnopqrstuvwxyz
ff fi fl ffi ffl 1234567890$.,-;'"?!()¿¡

**The purpose of good typography is to pre-
sent the message clearly and legibly for
fast, easy reading and comprehension. It
should also impart a smart, well-groomed
look that adds both appearance and appeal. A careful analysis of the purpose for**

Fig. 6-6 (reduced from actual size) Example of how a single type style (Vega) can vary in weight and shape. The letters "E" along the sides indicate the sizes available. The number next to the "E" is the size measured in points. *Courtesy Central Graphics, Inc., San Diego, CA.*

85

```
ABCDEFGHIJKLMNOPQRSTU
abcdefghijklmnopqrstuv  $123450
A— Roman

ABCDEFGHIJKLMNOPQR
abcdefghijklmnopqrstuvw
B— Gothic (Sans Serif)

ABCDEFGHIJKLMNOPQRST
ABCDEFGHIJKLMN $123456789
C— Square Serif

ABCDEFGHIJKLMNOPQRSTUVWXYZ
abcdefghijklmnopqrstuvw  $12345670
D— Script and Text

ABCDEFGHIJKLMNOPQR
STUVWXYZÇÆŒÅØÄÖ
E— Miscellaneous

TYPE CLASSIFICATIONS
```

Fig. 6–7 Type classifications: A—Roman; B—Gothic (Sans Serif); C—Square Serif; D—Script and Text; E—Miscellaneous

inch; 72 points, therefore, are equivalent to one inch (36 points = ½ inch, 18 points = ¼ inch). Type sizes range from 4 to 144 points with 6, 7, 8, 9, 10 and 12 the most common for body copy. In display type (headlines), 14, 16, 18, 24, 30, 36, 42, 60, and 72 points are popular sizes. "Leading," the space between lines of typeset copy, is also expressed in points—10 point Bodoni with 2 point leading, for example.

The pica expresses linear measurements of the width and/or depth of a typeset column or line. One pica is equivalent to 12 points; 6 picas equal 72 points (one inch). For instance, a given block of copy set in type would be referred to as being 18 picas (3 inches) wide by 42 picas (7 inches) deep.

If you are involved in preparing artwork for reproduction, you should have a working knowledge of the point and the pica units of measurement. Until you are, don't hesitate to use inches.

You don't have to be a type whiz to make your ads, mailers, and brochures look professional and still be easily readable. Always remember the primary rule of advertising: *Keep it simple.* Here are some easy-to-follow tips that can help:

1. Keep your type selection simple. Use only one type style— two at the very most. You can find plenty of variety within one style.

2. When using different typefaces, be sure they are either very similar or distinctly dissimilar in appearance; otherwise, it will look wrong to the reader.

3. Limit the width of your typeset columns to 40 characters, including spaces between words.

4. Break up long columns of type with subheads; set them in boldface or italics.

5. Indent the first line at the beginning of each paragraph.

6. Use italics (slanted letters) with care; their primary purpose is for emphasis and not to be read in a large mass.

7. Set your body copy in a 9 or 10 point size. Most publications use these sizes, and people have become accustomed to reading them.

8. Use one or two points of spacing (called "leading") between lines of copy. It'll help increase readability.

9. Choose slightly larger and heavier typefaces for headlines that will be printed in color; it makes up for the lack of black in the letters.

10. Don't use all capital letters in your headlines; more than a line or two of capital letters is difficult to read.

11. When you have to break your headline into more than one line, break it for meaning and not for fitting purposes.

12. Don't change type styles as you go from line to line, particularly in the headline: Treat it as a single typographic unit.

13. Avoid having type printed in reverse (white letters on black); it's hard to read, and the letters run the danger of filling in.

14. Resist the temptation to print your copy over photos or illustrations; letters imprinted over different shades of gray break up and can be extremely difficult to read.

15. Avoid the excessive use of condensed type faces. Large amounts of these give a cramped and crowded effect and are difficult to read.

If you follow these few easy rules, your type will do the job it was designed for—to be read.

NEWSPAPER
ADVERTISING

advantages and disadvantages

I read but one newspaper and that more for its advertisements than its news.

THOMAS JEFFERSON (1743–1862)

Mr. Jefferson was probably typical of many of today's newspaper readers. Although they may be presold on a product by other media, people buy where they live; and newspaper advertising tells them where a product is being sold and how much it will cost. According to the Newspaper Advertising Bureau, nearly three out of four men and women read a newspaper every weekday.

Louis T. Fischer, of Dancer Fitzgerald Sample, Inc., stated, "Newspapers, despite some research which says that people turn to radio or TV for quick information on current events, continue to provide people with most of their knowledge of the community, of politics, of sports and their contemporaries. Advertisers, both local and national are aware of this strength and take advantage of it through immediate action ads."

Newspapers offer other advantages to the advertiser:

1. The short leadtime—the period between the publication's deadline and the printing of an ad—necessary for inserting an advertisement allows the advertiser to prepare an ad one day and see it appear in print a couple of days later. For example, an appliance dealer located in a city undergoing a heat wave can advertise his or her line of airconditioners quickly, before the warm weather ends, to increase sales. And newspapers offer fast response to advertising; the local advertiser can anticipate customer reaction as soon as the ad appears. Results are heaviest the first day an ad appears and drop off rapidly each succeeding day.

2. In addition, newspapers offer local retailers circulation concentrated in their immediate selling area. The retail market is covered more completely and thoroughly by newspapers than by most other forms of advertising.

3. Newspaper advertising is also flexible. Ads can be large or small with as much or as little detail as the advertiser needs to get the message across, based on what he can afford. There is flexibility in positioning (placing the ad where it will do the most good). It can and should be inserted in a section of the newspaper appropriate for the advertised product (sports, business, women, real estate, or another special interest category).

4. Newspapers are the preferred medium for cooperative ad-

89

vertising, which is national advertising placed through local retail stores (see Chapter 2).

5. An increasing number of newspapers offer the use of color for those advertisers who feel it will increase the effectiveness of their advertising enough to justify the additional cost.

There are, however, disadvantages to newspapers:

1. Newspapers are read rapidly by the average reader. To be effective and catch the reader's attention, an ad has to be attractive, informative, brief, and to the point. Long copy should be used when detail is important, but the reader in a hurry won't waste time wading through a lot of whipped cream verbiage.

2. Newspaper reproduction is poor in quality compared to other printed forms of media. This is due to the coarse paper used and the high-speed method of printing. Photographs suffer the most in newspaper reproduction; therefore, photos with strong contrast—good black-and-white areas—should be used since they reproduce better. Thin type styles in small sizes should be avoided as they tend to smudge or break up during reproduction.

3. Newspapers are crowded with grocery ads from Wednesday to Friday, so a small ad scheduled to appear during this period can get lost among all the supermarket giants. Stay away from the food section unless you belong there.

There are two basic forms of newspaper advertisements: (1) "Display ads," which usually show the product and copy set up in any manner the advertiser may choose, comprise the bulk of newspaper advertising. (2) "Classified ads" (also known as "help wanted" ads), which restrict the advertiser as to position, size and style of type, and the use of illustrations. Both display and classified advertising are available to either local (retail) or national (general) advertisers.

how to measure advertising space

The "agate line" (also called a "line") is the standard unit of measure used by newspapers to sell advertising space. It refers to the advertising *space only;* the actual number of typeset lines appearing in an ad has no bearing on the measurement of its space. The newspaper sells pure blank space; what the advertiser puts into that space is another matter.

There are 14 agate lines to an inch within one column (see Figure 7–1). For example:

1. An ad 5 inches deep × 1 col. = 70 lines (5 × 14 × 1 = 70).
2. An ad 5 inches deep × 2 cols. = 140 lines (5 × 14 × 2 = 140).

I realize this may sound confusing, and you are probably tempted to skip it and go on to something else, but it's important that you understand how to use agate lines to measure advertising space. To see if you get the idea, test yourself on these few problems. The answers are at the end of this chapter.

COLUMN INCHES TO AGATE LINES CONVERSION TABLES

TOTAL LINES

Columns wide

Inches	1	2	3	4	5	6	7	8
1	14	28	42	56	70	84	98	112
2	28	56	84	112	140	168	196	224
3	42	84	126	168	210	252	294	336
4	56	112	168	224	280	336	392	448
5	70	140	210	280	350	420	490	560
6	84	168	252	336	420	504	588	672
7	98	196	294	392	490	588	686	784
8	112	224	336	448	560	672	784	896
9	126	252	378	504	630	756	882	1008
10	140	280	420	560	700	840	980	1120
11	154	308	462	616	770	924	1078	1232
12	168	336	504	672	840	1008	1176	1344
13	182	364	546	728	910	1092	1274	1456
14	196	392	588	784	980	1176	1372	1568
15	210	420	630	840	1050	1260	1470	1680
16	224	448	672	896	1120	1344	1568	1792
17	238	476	714	952	1190	1428	1666	1904
18	252	504	756	1008	1260	1512	1764	2016
19	266	532	798	1064	1330	1596	1862	2128
20	280	560	840	1120	1400	1680	1960	2240
21½	301	602	903	1204	1505	1806	2107	2408

Each ¼" add 4 lines per column
Each ½" add 7 lines per column
Each ¾" add 11 lines per column

DEPTH CONVERSION

Inches	Lines	Inches	Lines	Inches	Lines	Inches	Lines
1	14	6	84	11	154	15¾	221
1¼	18	6¼	88	11¼	158	16	224
1½	21	6½	91	11½	161	16¼	228
1¾	25	6¾	95	11¾	165	16½	231
2	28	7	98	12	168	16¾	235
2¼	32	7¼	102	12¼	172	17	238
2½	35	7½	105	12½	175	17¼	242
2¾	39	7¾	109	12¾	179	17½	245
3	42	8	112	13	182	17¾	249
3¼	46	8¼	116	13¼	186	18	252
3½	49	8½	119	13½	189	18¼	256
3¾	53	8¾	123	13¾	193	18½	259
4	56	9	126	14	196	18¾	263
4¼	60	9¼	130	14¼	200	19	266
4½	63	9½	133	14½	203	19¼	270
4¾	67	9¾	137	14¾	207	19½	273
5	70	10	140	15	210	19¾	277
5¼	74	10¼	144	15¼	214	20	280
5½	77	10½	147	15½	217	21½	301
5¾	81	10¾	151				

Fig. 7–1 Conversion table; column inches to agate lines.

Just remember, 14 agate lines equal one column inch. Now, go ahead and try these samples.

1. An ad 10 inches deep × 1 column equals _____ lines.
2. An ad 12 inches deep × 1 column equals _____ lines.
3. An ad 6 inches deep × 2 columns equals _____ lines.
4. An ad 8 inches deep × 4 columns equals _____ lines.

Check out your answers. If you have at least three out of the four correct, keep reading. If not, better go over this section again. It really is important.

how to figure ad space cost

Now that you can measure the size of an ad in agate lines, it is an easy matter to calculate an ad's cost. We use another formula, but don't panic, it's easy. Read along slowly. The formula for figuring advertising space is this:

$$\text{Agate Lines} \times \text{Line Rate} = \text{Ad Cost}$$

For instance, if you have a 2 inch by 1 inch column ad (28 lines) and the rate is $1.50 per line, the total cost would be $42. (28 × $1.50 = $42.). That wasn't too bad, was it?

Let's try another example. An ad that measures 5 inches deep (70 lines) by 3 columns and has a rate of $1.50 per line will cost $315. (70 × 3 = 210 × $1.50 = $315.). Got it? Good. Now try these few simple problems to make sure you have the hang of it.

1. An ad 280 lines deep × 1 column @ $1.50 costs $_____.
2. An ad 140 lines deep × 2 columns @ $1.50 costs $_____.
3. An ad 140 lines deep × 3 columns @ $1.50 costs $_____.
4. An ad 40 lines deep × 4 columns @ $1.86 costs $_____.

Check your answers with the solutions at the end of this chapter. As before, if you have three out of the four correct, we'll keep going.

the rate card—
a wealth of information

A newspaper's rate card contains all of the information an advertiser needs in order to set up an annual ad budget and decide on an appropriate advertising contract. The card includes rates, discounts, copy requirements, mechanical requirements, contract regulations, deadlines, and circulation figures, along with other useful information. You can get a copy of the newspaper's current rate card (without charge) from the publisher. The effective date of the rate card is printed on its front cover, and it's important to take note of it. If you have a rate card more than a few months old, better check to find out if the information is still in effect. If you need rate information for out-of-town newspapers, you can find it in the monthly edition of *Standard Rate & Data* (see Chapter 14) at your public library or contact the publication directly.

Newspapers offer the lowest possible advertising rates to those advertisers with a "space contract." The space contract is an agreement between the advertiser and a publication to abide by the current rate card for such space as the advertiser actually uses during the contract period, which is usually 12 months. If the advertiser's situation changes and all of the space contracted for isn't used, the publication will "short rate" (definition below) him or her. An advertiser with a contract not only gets the advantage of lower rates but in some cases is protected against rate increases during the term of the contract. Payment for the contracted space is not made in advance. As the space is used, the advertiser is billed, and payment is due at that time.

Some of the different rates a newspaper may offer are these:

Flat Rate: Flat rates apply when an advertiser pays the same rate per line whether 50 lines or 50,000 lines of space are used. There is no discount.

Open Rate: When an open rate is quoted, the advertiser knows it is open to discounts. The size of the discount depends on either the volume of lineage used or the frequency of ads run during a given period.

Combination Rate: When a newspaper publishes both a morning edition and a separate evening edition, the advertiser may purchase space in them individually or together at a special "combination rate." To earn the combination rate, the same ad must appear in both papers, usually within a seven-day period. Some newspapers require that the second ad follow the first immediately.

National Rate: The national rate is also called the "general display" rate and is paid by national advertisers. It is typically higher than the rate charged to local advertisers and normally allows a 15% commission to advertising agencies.

Local Rate: The local rate is also known as the "retail display" rate. Local advertisers pay this rate, which is usually lower than that paid by national advertisers. However, since local rates are lower, there are no agency commissions allowed. Retail display rates are available only to advertisers doing retailer-to-consumer business from their own retail outlet. Mail-order firms do not qualify.

Short Rate: If an advertiser fails to fulfill the space contract, he will be billed for the difference between the space contracted for and the actual space used. This is called "short rating," and the invoice sent at the end of the contract period is known as a "short rate" bill.

Rebates: Rebates are just the opposite of short rates. In the event an advertiser uses more space than was contracted for, an additional discount is earned. So, at the end of the contract period, the advertiser will be sent an earned rebate check instead of an invoice.

mechanical requirements for running an ad

Newspapers are printed by one or more of the following methods: offset lithography, rotogravure, or letterpress. Each of these methods is described in Chapter 6. The rate card will tell which printing method is used; look for it under "mechanical requirements."

The printing process used is of interest to the advertiser insofar as it dictates the type of material the newspaper needs, such as prints, negatives, engravings, mats, and so on to reproduce the ad. When in doubt as to what type of material to prepare, send the original artwork, and the newspaper will make the proper material it needs to print the ad. There is usually an extra charge for this service.

helpful services available from newspapers

To assist the advertiser who has to prepare his own advertising, newspapers provide copywriting, artwork, typesetting, and other services. These services are usually provided free or at a nominal charge. Just remember that the newspaper has a tremendous volume of work each day and may not be able to give your ad the kind of attention it may need. As the advertiser, you should make it a point to check each ad at every stage of development, from beginning to finish. You should especially be sure to proofread ads for typographical errors; it's not uncommon for an address, phone number, model number, or price to get screwed up. It is the advertiser's responsibility to catch any error and inform the publication so it may be corrected before the deadline.

positioning your advertising

Newspapers use the "pyramid" pattern of placement for positioning ads (see Figure 7–2). Ads are built up in a pyramid or stairlike arrangement on the side of the newspaper page to encourage continued reading of editorial matter.

When you feel that your advertisement must appear in a specific location within the paper, you can ask for, and usually get, a

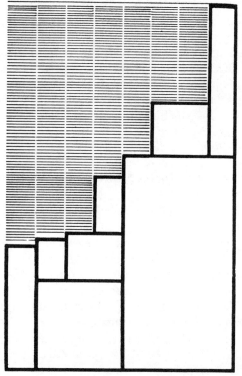

Fig. 7–2 Typical newspaper page make-up using the pyramid pattern of ad placement.

guaranteed "preferred position"; but you will be charged an additional amount for it.

When ad position is left to the discretion of the people who make up the paper, it's called "R.O.P.", or "run of paper," or "run of press." Avoid letting the newspaper personnel decide where to position your advertising. Newspaper make-up people are always fighting deadlines and may drop an ad in wherever it will conveniently fit. They just don't have the time to consider each ad thoughtfully and decide whether or not it logically belongs in a certain section. An ad can be buried so deep that only the advertiser's mother will find it.

Be specific about the position you want your advertising to have. When you want good placement but don't want to pay the extra charge for preferred position, request the position you desire and add the words, "urgently requested," on your order. The publication will try to honor your request, but they will not guarantee it.

If your ad appeals to a certain group, you can ask for and often get placement in a specific section of the newspaper. For example, if your ad is for men's slacks, request "sports section" or "business section." If you are selling garden supplies, ask to have your ad appear in the "real estate," "home," or "gardening" section. You can also request to have the ad placed "up front," or "above fold," or "next to reading matter."

Don't be casual about your ad's placement; a good position can increase readership. If you get stuck with a lousy position, call your newspaper sales rep and complain (the squeaky wheel gets the grease theory). I guarantee you'll get a better position and better results next time you run the ad.

ad shrinkage can shrink your budget

If you've noticed your ads seemed slightly smaller in size in print than the original artwork you submitted to the newspaper, don't run off to have your eyes checked. Ads do shrink in some newspapers. It's known as "shrinkage" and is due to the reproduction process used by some newspapers. In most cases, the size difference is negligible—only a fraction of an inch. This doesn't sound like much, but remember that you are paying for space by the line (14 agate lines to the column inch), and if your ad shrinks just two lines and is four columns wide, you have lost a total of eight lines (2 lines × 4 columns = 8 lines). If your rate is $1.50 per line, you would end up losing $12 ($1.50 × 8 = $12) in space you did not get. Let's go a step further. If you run the same size ad each week for a year (52 weeks), the cost of space lost to you would be $624 ($12 × 52 = $624).

There is, however, something you can do about ad shrinkage. You can compensate for shrinkage simply by making artwork for the original advertisement slightly larger than the printed reproduction size. If the newspaper you use is affected by shrinkage, get a layout or dimension sheet (see Figure 7–3). Ask your newspaper sales representative for this information.

Most papers will charge only for the space printed; but with the large volume of ads they process each day, measuring each produced ad and adjusting the invoice accordingly is not always possible. One way to handle this problem before the ad is printed is to include in your insertion order the phrase, "exact size to be determined by shrinkage of artwork," next to the size of the ad you intend to run. After the ad is printed, measure its size and check it against the newspaper's invoice to verify you are

Fig. 7–3 Newspaper mechanical specification chart.

WIDTH

Columns	Layout (or material) Width	Printed Width
1	1¾" — 10.9 picas	1⅝" — 9.9 picas
2	3⅝" — 22.0 picas	3¼" — 19.9 picas
3	5½" — 33.3 picas	4 15/16" — 29.9 picas
4	7⅜" — 44.6 picas	6 9/16" — 39.9 picas
5	9¼" — 55.9 picas	8¼" — 49.9 picas
6	11⅛" — 67.0 picas	9⅞" — 59.9 picas
7	13" — 78.3 picas	11½" — 69.9 picas
8	14⅞" — 89.9 picas	13¼" — 79.9 picas
12½ Double Truck	23⅛" — 139.0 picas	20 9/16" — 124.0 picas
14½ Double Truck	26⅞" — 161.6 picas	23⅞" — 144.0 picas
16½ Double Truck	30⅝" — 184.6 picas	27¼" — 164.0 picas

DEPTH

Layout (or Material) Depth Inches	Picas & Points	Printed Depth Inches	Agate Lines	Layout (or Material) Depth Inches	Picas & Points	Printed Depth Inches	Agate Lines
1	6.2	1	14	11 15/16	72.1	11½	161
1½	9.4	1½	21	12 7/16	75.3	12	168
2 1/16	12.6	2	28	13	78.5	12½	175
2 9/16	15.7	2½	35	13½	81.6	13	182
3 1/16	18.9	3	42	14	84.8	13½	189
3⅝	21.11	3½	49	14 9/16	87.10	14	196
4⅛	25.0	4	56	15 1/16	90.11	14½	203
4⅝	28.2	4½	63	15 9/16	94.1	15	210
5 3/16	31.4	5	70	16⅛	97.3	15½	217
5 11/16	34.5	5½	77	16⅝	100.4	16	224
6 3/16	37.7	6	84	17⅛	103.6	16½	231
6¾	40.9	6½	91	17 11/16	106.8	17	238
7¼	43.10	7	98	18 3/16	109.9	17½	245
7¾	47.0	7½	105	18¾	112.11	18	252
8 5/16	50.2	8	112	19¼	116.1	18½	259
8 13/16	53.3	8½	119	19¾	119.2	19	266
9 5/16	56.5	9	126	20 5/16	122.4	19½	273
9⅞	59.7	9½	133	20 13/16	125.6	20	280
10⅜	62.8	10	140	21 5/16	128.7	20½	287
10 15/16	65.10	10½	147	21⅞	131.9	21	294
11 7/16	69.0	11	154	22⅜	135.0	21½	301

getting what you are paying for in space. This simple precaution can keep your advertising budget from shrinking too.

make goods

Once in a while a newspaper will goof (no one's perfect) and print an ad so poorly that it can't be read. Or they may even run an ad on a wrong day—one other than that requested. When this happens, the publisher will make an adjustment. It's called a "make good." If it is justified, the newspaper will repeat the ad (called a "make good insertion") free of charge in the next possible issue. When repeating the ad is of no value to the advertiser—because of a time element, for instance—the paper, naturally, will not charge for what they did.

Occasionally an ad will appear poorly printed in only a few copies of the paper. A "make good," in this case, is probably not justified. Advertisers should be reasonable in their requests for make good insertions. Like everyone else in business, the publisher wants to keep customers satisfied and will do what is fair.

tear sheets

After an ad has been published in the newspaper, the page it appeared on will be sent to the advertiser as proof of publication. It is known as a "tear sheet" (rhymes with wear) and is normally accompanied by an invoice for the ad. The advertiser should look over the tear sheet and invoice carefully to make sure the ad ran as requested. Is the date right? Is the size correct? Were requested changes made? And so on.

In *Real Estate Agent*, J. Allen Thompson, of the *Atlanta Journal-Constitution*, reported,

> *One credit manager of a metropolitan newspaper told me that 10% of the advertisers get 50% of the credit adjustments. Why? Because they ask for it. In a newspaper, it's the squeaking wheel that gets the grease*
>
> *Errors will occur and in many cases they do no harm. When they do, however, and it is not your fault, you should not be timid in requesting a reasonable credit. In my opinion, an adjustment is due when the results of the ad were hurt.**

* From *The Real Estate Agent*, "How to Get More for Your Advertising Dollar" by J. Allen Thompson, November–December 1977, Heritage/Himmah Publications, Wellesley, MA.

how to get your ad in the paper

When you are ready to place your ad in a newspaper, you should send it in accompanied by a media "insertion order." An insertion order is similar to a company purchase order; it authorizes the publication to print your ad, and it includes all of the necessary instructions for doing it properly. The order may cover the placement of one or a series of ads. A form can be used (see Figure 7–4), or it may be typed on the advertiser's company letterhead. The following information should be included:

Fig. 7–4 Typical media insertion order you can use as a guide in preparing your own form.

YOUR COMPANY
NAME & ADDRESS

media order

DATE: J NO.:

MEDIA: CLIENT:

DESCRIPTION OF ADVERTISEMENT: _____

SIZE OR LENGTH: _____

POSITION OR PERIOD: _____

DATE(S) OF USE: _____

COMMISSION: _____

RATE(S): _____

DISCOUNT: _____

PRODUCTION DATA: _____

REMARKS _____

AUTHORIZED BY: _____

ALL INVOICES MUST BE SUBMITTED IN DUPLICATE AND TEAR SHEETS OR OTHER VERIFICATION OF APPEARANCE MUST BE ATTACHED.

1. Name and address of publication.
2. Date(s) when ad is to appear.
3. Title (or description) of advertisement.
4. Size of space authorized.
5. Position requested.
6. Rate you are paying.
7. Cash discounts or commissions to which you are entitled.
8. Type of production material you are sending to print from (artwork, print, negative, engraving, etc.).
9. Remarks, such as any additional information that is pertinent.
10. Name and title of person authorized to place the ad.

It's probably a good idea to include, on the insertion order, a request for all artwork to be returned to the advertiser.

If you want to run an ad that has appeared before, it can be easily repeated without sending new material by requesting the newspaper to "pick up ad run (date) on page (number)" in the insertion order.

deadlines can be deadly

The publication's deadline is the latest time you can get advertising material to the newspaper's offices in order to have your ad appear the day you specify. Obviously, it is better to plan ahead and get your material in early. But in some cases, this is not always possible, as the items you may want to feature won't be known or available until the very last minute. In a situation like this, it is particularly important to be aware of the deadline schedule. A schedule of deadline dates and times is available from the publisher; ask for a copy.

It is the advertiser's responsibility to get the ad material to the newspaper on time, not the publisher's. When the schedule calls for advertising materials to be in the newspaper's office by 4:00 P.M., that's exactly what is meant, not 4:01 P.M. When you are having material delivered to the paper's office, mark the outside of the envelope in large bold letters, "Advertising material on deadline—process immediately!" This precaution can keep material from sitting around, ignored, on someone's desk for a couple of hours.

classified advertising

Classified advertising has served as a kind of community bulletin board ever since advertising began. People use classified ads to buy, sell, locate, swap, bargain-hunt, compare, and promote products ranging in worth from a few cents to items, such as homes and cars, selling for many thousands of dollars.

Once thought of as an advertising medium for only automobile and real-estate sales, more and more retailers are finding the classified pages a relatively inexpensive way to sell soft goods, furniture, appliances, vocational training courses, or you name it.

A study by the Newspaper Advertising Bureau reports that seven out of ten families read the classified advertising pages in their daily newspaper. And six out of ten purchases from retailers were made through the classified columns of newspapers. Classified advertising is easy and fast; frequently the ad you place today can appear in tomorrow's paper. This convenience and immediacy are its main appeals.

However, classified ads do have their limitations. They are more restrictive than display ads, illustrations and photos are not allowed, and type is uniform as to size and style. The ads tend to look alike, although even this characteristic can be an advantage for the small advertiser, since he doesn't have to compete visually against his big-budget competition.

Some newspapers offer "classified display" space that, as the name implies, is a combination of classified and display advertising. This style of ad format appears either at the beginning or at the end of the classified section of the newspaper. Classified display ads are less restrictive and illustrations, different type styles, layouts, ornaments, and decorative borders are allowed.

Classified advertising space is sold by the line, by the word, or by the inch—depending on the newspaper's policy. There are two types of rates, "local" and "national," similar to display advertising. Local classified rates apply to advertisers doing business within a given local geographic area. This rate is noncommissionable and is normally lower than the national rate. Yearly contracts are available, with discounts for frequency or volume of lineage allowed.

National classified rates apply to those advertisers outside the local geographic area, and they are usually 15% commissionable to qualified advertising agencies. An additional cash discount of 2% may also be offered if payment is made within ten days.

To estimate the cost of placing your classified ad, here's an easy formula to follow: It's called "Five by Five." It's simple. First, write out your ad. Then count the number of words (using five characters per word). If your paper charges by the word, take the total number of words and multiply by the word cost. If the paper charges by the line, divide the total number of words by five (the number of words to a line) and then multiply by the line rate. Either way you calculate will give you a fair approximation of the cost.

When you submit a classified ad for insertion, it's a good idea to have the copy accurately typewritten beforehand. The newspaper will set the copy in type at no extra charge, but advertisers have very little selection in the matter. Advertisers are required to check their ad on the first day of publication and report any errors. The newspaper is not normally responsible for more than one incorrect insertion and will usually adjust any error on their part by a corrected insertion for that one time. Be sure to check and double-check your ad as soon as it appears.

There are no preferred positions in the classified section. An ad will automatically appear in the appropriate category suggested by the advertised offer.

But there are a variety of classifications from which the businessperson can choose. For example, there are headings for Florists, Home Improvements, Moving & Storage, Painting & Decorating, Travel, Swimming Pool & Spa Construction, and Furniture. There are also sections for merchandise, such as Business Equipment, Carpets & Drapes, Jewelry, Household Appliances, Radio–Television, Sporting Goods, Stereo & Hi-Fi, and Thrifties for the bargain hunters. Popular classifications like Real Estate and Automotive offer many, many sub-classifications. A direct mail advertiser can order "reader reply" box numbers included in the ad. When the responses come to the newspaper, they will hold them for pickup or send them on to the advertiser, for an additional charge.

A very important thing to remember about people who read classified ads is that they are doing so for a purpose. They have something in mind that they need and want. For this reason, they are excellent prospects, since they are likely to react quickly to a well-presented sales message.

When writing a classified ad, remember that the same rules apply as in other forms of advertising. The reader wants information, so be as specific as you can and include all pertinent data. Be factual and imaginative. Write the message so your words are clear and brief, simple and truthful. Avoid overused words and trite clichés. Keep the whole message easy to read. Don't use hard-to-abbreviate words, and don't try to abbreviate too much; if the reader has to spend time decoding your message, you'll probably lose him or her. And in most cases, you'll find it a good idea to include the price of your product or service.

Moderate cost and quick results make classified advertising a valuable advertising form. If you haven't used it before, try it out. And be sure to keep a record of your results.

newspaper layout and copy checklist

This layout and copy checklist* has been prepared after analyzing thousands of newspaper merchandise ads for strong and weak points. Of course, even the best checklist can only do so much. It can't guarantee great advertising. But it can help you improve the overall quality of your ads. And it can help you avoid making really bad errors.

Specifically, the checklist will enable you to take an objective look at any ad you've done and discover any weaknesses the ad has. It will also suggest ways to improve any weaknesses you find.

general

1. Is there a dominant illustration or headline that instantly telegraphs the message?

The newspaper reader should be able to tell at a glance what your ad is about. People read the ads because they're interested in what stores have to sell. So be sure they know what your ad is selling by telegraphing the message with a dominant illustration or headline.

2. Is the ad suitable for good newspaper reproduction?

Will the illustration and copy print clearly or will they be blurred? Is the illustration style suitable for your newspaper, or should it be changed for better reproduction? One rule: Never run body copy in reverse or superimposed over a halftone.

3. Does the ad have a distinctive, recognizable format?

Would your readers—especially the store's regular customers—recognize the ad even without the store name? Example: the highly visible format developed by B. Altman. It adds extra impact and recognition to the store's small-space ads.

* Checklist produced by the Newspaper Advertising Bureau for the International Newspaper Advertising Executives. Reprinted with permission.

4. Does the ad have a recognizable logo?

The logo should include the store's name, address and telephone number—at least—plus other pertinent information which you want to run in every ad, such as store hours, credit information, etc.

layout

5. Is the ad well-organized and easy to follow?

A poorly organized layout makes things difficult for the reader. This is especially true for ads with many items of merchandise, where a well-organized layout with a headline that applies to all the items adds up to an inviting presentation of merchandise.

6. Does the ad have a clean, uncluttered look?

Many people's first impression of a store is from its advertising. Does the ad make a good impression . . . and is the merchandise in the ad easy to find?

7. Is more white space needed?

White space is probably the most underestimated element in newspaper advertising. Consider using more white space; it pays off in attention value.

8. Does the illustration demonstrate a benefit or show the merchandise in use?

This helps the reader *visualize* herself or himself using the product—and this is an important step toward making the sale. Apparel ads are usually more effective when they show the merchandise being worn.

9. Is the illustration large enough?

Research shows that ads with large merchandise pictures get higher readership than ads with small illustrations or with no illustration. People want to *see* the merchandise you're selling.

copy

10. Is the headline aimed at the target audience?

This helps assure you of reaching everyone who is in the market for what you have to sell. Be sure your prospects know you're talking to them.

11. Are there benefits or news in the headline?

A benefit is what the merchandise does for the reader—in other words, benefits are what make people buy things. If your headline doesn't give the reader at least one good reason to buy, write another headline.

12. Is the copy written in terms of benefits?

Spell out in detail what he or she will get from the merchandise you're selling. Make the reader feel your merchandise will *do things* for him or her.

13. Is the copy complete and specific?

Your copy should be complete enough, with enough details, so that a reader can pick up the phone and call in an order with confidence.

14. Is the language simple and direct?

Your copy should read like conversation. Try reading it aloud and see how it sounds. If it doesn't sound so good, try using shorter sentences and simpler words.

15. Are the prices clear and visible?

Most newspaper readers are interested in prices when they're shopping the ads. Make sure they don't have trouble finding them.

16. Is the reader urged to act immediately?

Every ad should include a strong bid for action on the reader's part. It's an essential part of closing the sale.

For more information on all aspects of advertising in newspapers, write to the Newspaper Advertising Bureau, Inc., 485 Lexington Avenue, New York, New York 10017, for a list of their publications.

solutions to problems

Page 92, Agate lines: 1. 140; 2. 168; 3. 168; 4. 448.
Page 92, Space cost: 1. $420; 2. $420; 3. $630; 4. $297.60.

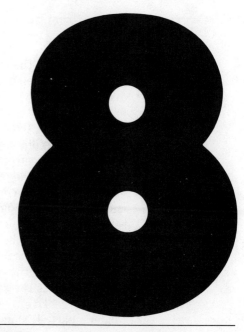

MAGAZINES

consumer magazines— popular with the public

The advantages of magazine advertising are many and make it an important medium for you to consider. According to *Standard Rate & Data Service*, "Magazines are the national medium for advertisers, big and small. . . . Over the nation, magazines are read in better than eight out of every ten homes in every sales area." And according to the Magazine Publisher's Association, the following reasons have helped make magazines a favorite medium for advertisers:

1. *Authority*. Magazine authority dates back to man's very acceptance of the printed word as dependable.
2. *Color*. Magazine color spreads a spectrum of exciting visual pleasure before the reader.
3. *Believability*. Magazine believability builds reader confidence.
4. *Permanence*. Magazines last. People save them—put them aside for future reference.
5. *Selectivity*. Magazine selectivity targets places and people.
6. *Flexibility*. Magazines offer a full range of prospects with divergent interests.

Let's look first at "consumer magazines." They are those magazines directed to the general public, or one or more segments of the public, as differentiated from trade, business, or industrial publications.
  There are two basic types of consumer magazines: (1) general and (2) special interest. The editorial content of a magazine determines the type and class of its readership; *House Beautiful* is written for the homeowner, whereas *Sports Illustrated* is designed for the sportsperson.

General Magazines: Reader's Digest, Time, Saturday Evening Post, Life, People Weekly, etc., are edited for the mass market, with resulting large circulations, and reach a broad cross-section of the population throughout the country. This type of magazine is ideally suited for advertising products with widespread appeal—automobiles, beverages, remedies, toothpaste, frozen foods, and so on—sold nationally.

Special Interest Magazines: Road & Track, Golf, Coin World, Flying, Popular Photography, etc., are written for specific groups of people who have common interests or hobbies. The specialized editorial content assures an advertiser of reaching readers who are logical prospects, without wasted circulation. If you were promoting a new type of exerciser for tennis players, for example, *Tennis* magazine and *World Tennis* would be logical publications for your ad. Actually, you would be hard pressed to name a class or type of people that is not served wholly or partially by at least one special interest magazine. Standard Rate & Data Service (SRDS) lists 51 different classifications from "Arts & Antiques" to "Youth."

Metropolitan Magazines: Another form of consumer magazine is the "metropolitan" publication, edited for the residents of a particular city or community. The title is often the name of the city or area where the magazine is published and distributed (Atlanta, Chicago, Dallas, Cleveland, and San Diego magazines, just to name a few). The editorial content of metro magazines deals with cultural and economic subjects of local concern. Metro magazines offer the local advertiser an opportunity to reach those people within his or her own selling area.

"Visitor" Magazines: These are still another form of local, special interest publications, and they are geared to the needs of the visiting tourist. Visitor publications list local attractions, hotel and motel accommodations, recreation areas, restaurants, theaters, and the like.

Geographical Editions of National Consumer Magazines: Such publications have geographic editions and may cover several states, a single state, or a large city, including its surrounding suburbs. An advertiser can appear in a national publication, such as *Business Week, Family Circle, Fortune, House Beautiful, Redbook Magazine, TV Guide,* or *Time,* and only pay for those regions in which the ad actually runs. For example, you could advertise a full-page, black-and-white advertisement in the total circulation of *TV Guide* for $58,800 (1980 rates), or you could choose to run the same ad in *TV Guide's* Eastern New England edition for only $2,100 (1980). The circulation, of course, is much smaller; but if that's where you're located, you don't care about the readers in Arizona. A few publications offer demographic editions, which are a selection of readers by occupation, such as doctors and college people.

There are a number of reasons you should think about magazine advertising. One of the major advantages of a consumer magazine is its long life. People seldom read a magazine from cover to cover in one sitting. A magazine is usually picked up at leisure and referred to several times before it is discarded by the owner, offering the advertiser more than one chance to have the advertising message read. Weekly magazines remain in a recipient's home for at least a week, whereas monthly magazines boast a longevity of from one month to a year. If you have ever spent time in a doctor's waiting room, you can appreciate this claim to endurance. Magazine ads that include a coupon continue to pull responses long after the ad has appeared. Mail-order advertisers are not surprised to receive an occasional coupon a year after its initial appearance.

For the advertiser whose product would be enhanced by the use of color (food, cosmetics, jewelry, paints, etc.), magazines have a faithfulness of reproduction unequaled by no other medium. Although television can handsomely display a product in color, the projected image and mood are gone in a few short seconds. In a magazine, the reader can unhurriedly romanticize over a colorful display of cruise-ship activities and dream about the pleasures of shipboard life.

When you're considering placing an advertisement in a consumer magazine, knowing where to find the information you will need is no problem. You can get everything you require from a publication's "rate card."

Rate cards, supplied free to prospective advertisers, contain complete data regarding space rates, special discounts, sizes of space available, mechanical requirements for producing the ad, closing dates (deadlines), issue dates (when the publication will appear), and circulation figures.

In addition, most publications have "media kits" available, also yours for the asking. They contain detailed, audited circulation figures, geographical circulation breakdowns, and demographic studies as to the type of reader reached by the publication.

The rate card has three dates that are important to you, the advertiser. (1) The Cover Date—which, as the name implies, is the date (month) printed on the cover of a publication. (2) The On-Sale Date—the actual date the magazine appears on newsstands or reaches its subscribers. Magazines usually appear on sale in advance of the cover date. A magazine with a cover date of April could be on the newsstands as early as March 10th, for example. (3) The Closing Date (also called the "Deadline")—the last day on which a magazine will accept an advertisement to guarantee its appearance in a specific issue. On the average, weekly magazines close two to three weeks prior to publication, whereas a monthly magazine may close one to three months before it goes on sale. Some magazines will accept an ad after the closing date for an additional 10% of the going rate. Extensions of the closing date may be possible; if you're in a bind, try asking for an extension.

Check the rate card for the publication's "mechanical requirements" to determine what type of printing material (litho negatives, engravings, photoprints, etc.) the magazine requires in order to reproduce your ad. You can also find out what halftone screens (see Chapter 6) are acceptable and what, if any, restrictions a magazine may have regarding the use of solid black areas.

Have camera-ready artwork (see Chapter 4) prepared so it fits the exact size ad space indicated in the rate card. An ad that does not meet the publication's specifications may be refused.

Remember that your magazine ad will be seen for some time. Take care in the preparation; create it to reflect the quality you represent. Also, watch your timing—closing dates can be early. And, above all, keep it simple (you've heard that before). A good magazine ad will work for you for weeks, months, and maybe even years.

understanding magazine space and rates

Advertising is to business what steam is to machinery—the great propelling power.

THOMAS MacCAULEY (1800–1859)

For someone who grew up during the early 1800s, when advertising was just getting started, Mr. MacCauley was a pretty far-sighted individual. He must have been impressed with the few magazines appearing at the time and could imagine the potential "great propelling power" they had for manufacturers and retailers who had new products to sell. With the advent of the industrial revolution and, later, with the development of mass production, it was inevitable magazines would grow as fast as the new companies (Ford Motor Company, Procter and Gamble, General Foods) that began advertising within their pages.

Advertisers have magazines available to them that are directed to all types of audiences and special interest groups on a weekly, bi-weekly, monthly, bi-monthly, seasonal, quarterly, or annual basis.

Although there are different sizes of magazines—small (*Reader's Digest*) and large *(Life)*—the standard page size is 8½ × 11 inches (*Time* magazine). The standard page ad size (called the type area) is 7 × 10 inches. Ads that extend to the edge of the paper, beyond the margin, are known as "Bleed Pages."

Magazine space is normally sold in units of a full page or fractions of pages (half page, one-third page, one-quarter page, three columns, two columns, one column, etc.). Some periodicals offer space by the agate line (14 agate lines equal one inch), similar to newspapers; line rates are used by advertisers with small ads.

Rates are based on the guaranteed number of copies a magazine distributes; it's known as the "circulation rate base." The circulation figures of most large periodicals are verified by either the Audit Bureau of Circulation (ABC Reports) or the Business Publications Audit of Circulation (B.P.A.); both are nonprofit independent auditing organizations.

The most prominent spots for magazine advertising are the covers. Magazine covers are identified as first (front) cover, second (inside front) cover, third (inside back) cover, and fourth (back) cover. The front cover traditionally does not carry any advertising, but the other covers are available and are considered desirable by advertisers who pay premium rates for the space.

Magazine rates are usually discounted in one of two ways, by volume or by frequency. Volume discounts are based on the total amount of space an advertiser uses during a given period. The ads may be of different sizes and run at different times, but it is the total amount of space used that determines the discount earned. Frequency discounts are based on the total number of insertions by an advertiser on a regular basis (3 ads in a year, 6 ads a year, etc.). The total amount of space purchased has no effect on the discount earned. Frequency discounts are offered more than volume discounts by most magazines.

Additional charges are added to the base rate for bleed or color ads and for preferred position pages.

Ordering magazine space is a two-step process. First, a contract has to be signed by the advertiser. It states the rate the advertiser will pay for whatever space will be used during the contract period (normally, 12 months). And secondly, an insertion order has to be sent with each ad prior to the time it is to appear. It contains instructions from the advertiser to the publication for placing individual ads. Normally, the advertising space contract is sent to the publication with the first insertion order.

If you contract for a certain amount of space but use less than that amount, you will be "short rated." This is a bill for the difference between space contracted for and space actually used. However, if you purchase more space than was contracted for—enough to earn a lower rate—the publication will happily offer a rebate. The rebate is generally in the form of an adjustment on the cost of the last ad to appear during the contract period.

A word of caution: Although the majority of magazine publications offer short rates and rebates, a few do not. They consider their contracts noncancellable and will hold the advertiser liable for completion. Before you sign a contract, be sure you understand what your obligations are and what flexibility you do or don't have.

In their rate cards, publishers refer to two types of circulation, "Primary" and "Pass-Along." Primary circulation is the actual number of people who receive a magazine, whether by subscription, purchase, or however. The pass-along circulation is an estimate as to how many other people besides the primary reader also read the periodical. Publishers rationalize that since a magazine stays around a home, office, or reception room area for 30 days, it is bound to be read by people other than the primary reader. A valid point for most estimates, but it's obviously open to exaggeration. I suggest you use the primary circulation figure when considering a magazine and regard the pass-along circulation as a fringe benefit.

A few points to remember when considering magazine advertising are the following:

1. There are publications directed toward special interest groups with which you can reach people who are interested in your particular product or service.

2. Magazines will usually stay around for some time, giving your ad a bit more exposure.

3. You may save some money by taking advantage of frequency or volume discounts.

seven suggestions for better business advertising

Earlier, I talked about consumer magazine advertising, but what if you are trying to reach some of the millions of people involved in business and industry? You can reach them faster and cheaper by advertising in business publications than by any other method. The American Business Press Association estimates that 8 out of 10 businesspeople read one or more specialized business magazines related to their profession on a regular basis. Businesspeople are seriously interested in any new idea, product, equipment, material, or information that will help them to do a better job and/or increase profits. Harry S Truman (1884–1973) knew this when he said, "Advertising has induced progress in the use of new materials, new tools, and new processes of manufacture by calling attention to their economies." For this reason, the advertising within business publications often is as well read for its information as is the magazine's editorial content. The main advantage of a business magazine is its ability to reach a specific audience. And since business markets are smaller than consumer markets, it is possible for the advertiser to reach most potential customers in relatively few publications.

For ease of identification, business magazines can be divided into three categories: (1) general business publications, (2) specialized business magazines, (3) farm publications.

General Business Publications: Nation's Business, Business Week, Fortune, Forbes, etc., are aimed at executives in top-level management positions. In most of these publications, the editorial content covers all industries on a national basis. If you're trying to reach the really big people, these are probably your best bet.

Specialized Business Publications: These are referred to as "trade" papers. When directed to a single industry, they are called vertical publications; *The Iron Age, Oil & Gas Journal*, and *Datamation* are some examples. If the specialized business publication is geared to professional people with similar occupations but working in different industries, they are called horizontal publications; examples include *Administrative Management, Engineering Digest*, and *Successful Selling*. Trade papers can be further classified as (1) industrial (manufacturing, construction, research & development, etc.); (2) trade (retailing, wholesaling, supplies, marketing, etc.); and (3) professional (engineering, chemical, medical, sales, etc.).

Farm Publications: These supply a combination of business and home-oriented information to the modern farmer. Most are rather sophisticated and carry the latest technical information of importance to today's farmer, such as computerized farming methods, scientific breeding, chemical applications, and environmental engineering. Many are written for a specific region where climate and soil conditions have similar effects on plant and animal life.

Some business publications send free subscriptions to selected people within a particular industry; it's called "controlled circulation." Critics argue that recipients are less likely to read them than they would paid-subscription publications. Advocates reason that such circulation is the only way to assure coverage of the market.

Also, many business publications have postage-free,

reader-service, or "bingo" cards inserted in the magazine. A reader desiring more information on an article or advertisement can check a keyed number on the card and return it to the publication. The magazine forwards the request to the appropriate company who, in turn, sends the information to the individual requesting it. There is an advantage and disadvantage to bingo cards; it's a case of quantity versus quality. Although bingo cards can produce a high volume of leads, the quality can be of low caliber. Students, competitors, collectors, and so on, who have no serious intent to purchase, have to be weeded out, which can be time consuming and expensive.

Advertising space in business publications is sold on a volume (total amount of space) or frequency (total number of ads) basis. Generally, space is sold in full or fractional page units. A few publications, mostly tabloid size, sell space by the agate line (14 lines deep by one column wide equals one column inch, similar to newspapers). You can find detailed information in the rate card, available from the publisher, or in monthly editions of Standard Rate & Date Service (see Chapter 14), which are available by subscription or in the reference section of the public library.

When preparing your ad for a business publication, remember that the reader is interested in news and information. To increase the effectiveness of your ad, use the following guidelines to help you.

1. Feature product benefits that will help the reader's business or occupation. Explain how your product can save time or money; a product that can reduce costs by even a fraction of a cent per unit can mean savings of thousands of dollars in mass production.

2. Feature new applications of your product that will be of interest; use photos with captions to explain the technical advantages clearly.

3. Don't be afraid to write long factual copy; if it's relevant, it will be read. Break up long columns of type with subheadings in order to highlight main points for the reader who is just glancing. Set key paragraphs in bold type.

4. Design the ad to resemble editorial matter: It can increase readership.

5. Be specific. "The new Widget can reduce production time 15%," is better than "It saves time."

6. Keep your message simple: business readers don't have time to waste deciphering complex ideas.

7. Use color functionally: Splashing color over an ad without purpose won't increase readership. Stay black and white and save the extra costs.

how effective is advertising?

Recently I came across a series of advertising research reports, produced by the Cahners Publishing Company, 221 Columbus Avenue, Boston, Massachusetts 02116, which deal with a subject all advertisers are concerned with—advertising effectiveness. They looked interesting, so I thought I'd pass them on to you.

1. how is advertising readership influenced by ad size?

Purpose: To determine the relative advantages of the utilization of larger sized advertisements to communicate an advertising message.

Methodology: Cahners Research analyzed 2,353 advertisements. The ads were sorted by size classification and indexed against the overall average.*

AD SIZE	INDEX SCORE
2 pages	213
1 page	124
⅔ page	94
½ page	91
⅓ page	66
¼ page	55

Conclusion: As the size of an advertisement increases, the readership score increases. Two-page ads received scores more than twice as high as the average, while ¼-page ads scored 45% lower than the average.

2. what is the average number of inquiries generated by ad size?

Purpose: To determine the average number of inquiries generated by ad size.

* An index score is used when comparisons against "average" are important. In this instance, the average for all ads studied is converted to a base of 100, and all scores are weighted against this index.

115

Methodology: Cahners Research analyzed 500,000 inquiries generated by *Design News, EDN,* and *Plastics World.* These inquiries were then slotted by ad size and averaged across all ads.

AD SIZE	INQUIRIES
Full page	119
⅔ page	103
½ page	101
⅓ page	82
¼ page	92

Conclusion: Inquires, on the average, will increase as the size of the advertisement increases. Obviously, the type of audience reached and the content of the advertisement play a major role in the number of inquiries generated. Certain audiences do not inquire at all. This data makes no attempt to analyze the qualitative aspects of audience or advertisement.

3. what is the cost of an average inquiry by ad size?

Purpose: To determine the cost of an average inquiry by the size of the ad.

Methodology: Cahners Research analyzed 500,000 inquiries generated by *Design News, EDN,* and *Plastics World.* These inquiries were sorted by ad size and averaged across all ads. The resulting numbers were then divided into the average rate for each size ad to arrive at the cost per inquiry.

SIZE OF AD	INQUIRIES	COST PER INQUIRY
Full page	119	$20.44
⅔ page	103	17.45
½ page	101	14.14
⅓ page	82	11.37
¼ page	92	7.97

Conclusion: While the number of inquiries increases as the size of the advertisement increases, the cost per inquiry increases as well.

Obviously, the type of audience reached and the content of the advertisement play a major role in the number of inquiries generated. Certain audiences do not inquire at all. This data makes no attempt to analyze the qualitative aspects of audience or advertisement.

4. how long do advertisements draw inquiries?

Purpose: To determine how long an advertisement in a specialized business magazine draws inquiries.

Methodology: Cahners Research analyzed over 175,000 inquiries generated by advertisements in 5 selected publications with 10-week inquiry processing cycles. All inquiries were charted on a weekly basis.

WEEK	INQUIRIES (CUMULATIVE)
1	4,762
2	10,999
3	16,362
4	17,838
5	19,484
6	20,277
7	21,001
8	21,354
9	21,654
10	21,854

Conclusion: On the average, the greatest number of inquiries are generated in the last 4 weeks of processing—practically 50% of the total. The first 3 weeks represent the least activity—less than 20%.

5. do inquiries lead to sales?

Purpose: To determine the actions which are taken by inquirers after they have received the requested information.

Methodology: Three separate studies were conducted, totaling 9,200 inquiries. Specific questions were included to determine "what happened" after the material was received.

50%—building a reference file
25%—decided on a competitor's product
12½%—bought or specified ad product
12½%—are potential purchasers

Conclusion: Based on 4,381 replies, fully half the respondents had an immediate application in mind, and half the respondents used the material for reference or file. Over 12% of all respondents bought or specified the advertised product.

As I mentioned, these statistics looked interesting, and you may find them useful in planning your advertising. When used properly, percentages, averages, and statistics can be a good basis for planning. It's always good to remember, however, "the man who drowned crossing a stream with an average depth of six inches."

one-for-one deals in magazines

If your advertising plans include magazines, you might be eligible for a free editorial write-up.

Some magazines, if asked, will run one free editorial for one paid advertisement; it's called a "one-for-one" deal. Other publications allow one free editorial for every two ads placed (a "one-for-two" deal). The national consumer and trade magazines that have this unwritten policy of advertising backscratching don't promote it. In fact, they may even deny this type of thing is being done. But don't believe everything they say. You can see for yourself; just look in the "new products" or "mail order" sections of several publications, and you'll discover the companies running ads are usually the same ones that have items featured in the editorial columns. Mail-order advertisers, in particular, insist on and consistently get these freebies.

Try it! What have you got to lose? There are enough magazines offering these one-for-one deals to make it worth your while to do a little wheeling and dealing. Ask your magazine sales representative to handle it for you. Your rep will probably not guarantee anything but will be happy to accept your order for a paid ad and agree to pass on your product write-up to the editor with a recommendation for a free editorial. You could end up with, in effect, two ads for the price of one. And that, you must agree, is a bargain anytime.

RADIO
AND TELEVISION

radio—a sound medium

"Return with us now, to those thrilling days of yesteryear. From out of the past comes the thundering hoofbeats of the great horse, Silver." If you're my age, you probably recall those exciting words announcing the arrival of the Lone Ranger on radio. It was radio's heyday. Even though Tonto, Jack Armstrong, Lamont Cranston and his aide, the lovely Margo Lane, are all gone, radio is still alive and well. In 1945 there were fewer than 1,000 radio stations; today there are over 4,500.

Radioman David Field, in *MAC*, commented that "radio is getting it 'good' from both ends. That is, small advertisers who have used newspapers are going into radio because they can sound as good as a national advertiser; large budget advertisers who normally concentrate on TV are frightened by its cost and returning to radio."

There may be only one newspaper in a typical city, but there are usually many, many more radio stations. There are stations directed to selective audiences—teenagers, adults, housewives, minority groups, farmers, foreign-language-speaking people, and religious groups. There are stations with programming that includes classical, contemporary, country, western, and standard music, and there are those that feature news, sports, interviews, or special events. By catering to specific audiences, radio offers an advertiser the opportunity to pinpoint his or her message to a special group.

Like television, radio is sold in 10-, 30-, and 60-second spot increments. Rates vary, depending on the size of audience a station can deliver and the time of day. Radio prime time is during morning hours and late afternoon—commuter driving times. For the purpose of selling time, the broadcast day is divided and classified into segments. A typical breakdown would be:

Class AA	6:00 A.M. to 10:00 A.M.	(Drive time)
B	10:00 A.M. to 4:00 P.M.	(Daytime)
A	4:00 P.M. to 7:00 P.M.	(Drive time)
C	7:00 P.M. to Midnight	(Evening)
	Midnight to 6:00 A.M.	(Late night)

Class AA is considered the prime time period and is, therefore, the most expensive. Class D would be the least expensive time to advertise.

Although rates are published, purchasing radio time can be negotiated. Policies may vary from station to station, but discounts are available. The most common are frequency discounts (based on the number of spots purchased) and volume discounts (based on the total dollars spent).

120

Package plans are also offered. They allow the advertiser a number of time slots at various times during the day, usually over a period of a week, at a special flat price. It's called a Total Audience Plan (T.A.P.) and is usually a good buy, if it fits the advertiser's needs. As I said, rates are negotiable, but they will frequently depend on the buyer's bargaining ability. If you're spending a lot of money on radio, you have some leverage.

Remember that radio is a short-lived medium. The message goes in one ear and out the other. To make any kind of an impact on the listener, the commercial should run frequently. Does that mean you have to be on the air every day? No, but you should plan the time carefully and concentrate your commercials to saturate a certain time period, such as weekends or every day during a sale period, for example.

Radio is a very flexible medium. Commercials and schedules can easily be changed on short notice to take advantage of changes in news events or the weather. In the summer when television viewing falls off, radio audiences increase, which could make it a better buy.

fourteen suggestions
for more effective radio commercials

Radio commercials are easy and relatively inexpensive to produce (see Figure 9–1). However, because it is an aural (sound) medium, the techniques are different from those used in print media. Here are some helpful hints based on research developed by the Radio Advertising Bureau:

1. Use short, easy-to-understand words and sentences; avoid tongue-twisters.
2. Use imagination in your words, voices, and sounds to create mental pictures in the listener's mind. In an ad for the *Wall Street Journal*, adman Bob Gage of Doyle Dane Bernbach said, "You have to hit 'em where their heart is. You can sell far more if you're emotional rather than intellectual."
3. Avoid promoting many different items; radio is strongest for one-theme ideas, such as a "weekend sale, now going on."
4. Radio is a very intimate medium; people tend to listen alone. Talk directly to the listener and use words like "you" often; be sincere, believable, warm, and friendly.
5. Mention your name at the beginning, middle, and end of each commercial. Radio is often used in the background while a person is working or reading. The commercial must break through this mental activity.

```
                        N W Ayer /A\B\H\ International
                           1345 Avenue Of The Americas, New York, N. Y. 10019

   CLIENT    AT&T LONG LINES                PROGRAM

   PRODUCT   LONG DISTANCE                  FACILITIES

   TITLE     "SANDI"                        DATE     12/13/78

   NUMBER    as Produced AXLL3724           LENGTH   :30 Radio
```

> SFX OF TELEPHONE AS HEARD THROUGH A TELEPHONE EARPIECE.
>
> SANDI: (FILTERED) Hi, this is Sandi...
>
> ANNCR: Sandi Pelouze tells about calling her mother
>
>   Long Distance.
>
> MUSIC BEGINS.
>
> SANDI: The day I got to hear the baby's heartbeat, I was
>
>   so excited, so I called my mother in Ohio. "Hey,
>
>   Mom. I can hear your new granddaughter she's
>
>   moving around." Just the sound of the heartbeat
>
>   and being able to express it with mom over the
>
>   phone was really something special.
>
> ANNCR: There's no better way to keep in touch than
>
>   Long Distance. Long Distance is the next
>
>   best thing to being there.
>
>   The Bell System.
>
> SINGER: Feelings...

Fig. 9–1 Typical radio script format. *Courtesy AT&T Long Lines Department.*

      6. As in other forms of advertising, appeal to the listener's self-interest. Offer a benefit or some real news.

      7. Direct your message to a specific group: housewives, young adults, commuters, and so on. For instance, commuters are good prospects for auto products, tires, tune-ups, car washes, and the like.

      8. Include a call to action—"Come in today" or "Call now."

Radio listeners are used to calling a station with requests for music or to participate in interview shows.

9. Have a series of different commercials ready for use. Create special ones for minority and ethnic groups.

10. Have whoever prepared the commercial read it to you with all of its inflections and emotions. Better yet, before you approve it, have a tape made and listen to the commercial as it will go over the air.

11. Use radio personalities if they are available and if their style fits your message. Many disc jockeys and announcers have loyal followings. Don't give them a prepared script; provide a fact sheet and let them "wing it."

12. Identify your product or service with a musical jingle or a personality or by distinctive dialogue. Repetition will build product identification.

13. If you have television commercials running during the same period, use the soundtrack or identical theme for added recall value.

14. Humor can be used very effectively if it's done well. But watch your timing; people tire of the same old joke quickly.

Remember that radio's strength lies in its unique ability to create mental images in the listener's mind. So use plenty of imagination to produce those "lip-smacking," "thirst-quenching" commercials.

television commercials— how to stand out from all that visual clutter

Television commercials pass before viewers with all the sight, sound, color, excitement, and pageantry of a never-ending three-ring circus on parade. In a typical household, the television set is turned on an average of over 6 hours a day (that's what the research people estimate). An interesting point to consider is that the allowable commercial time during the daytime period is 16 minutes per hour and 9½ minutes during the prime evening time. The poor viewer is bombarded with an estimated 20,000 commercials each year, creating what is known in the trade as "clutter." Clutter is the overabundance of advertising messages promoting everything from hair sprays, underarm sprays, odor sprays, mouth sprays, nose sprays, and foot sprays to fast foods, instant foods, prepackaged foods, ready-made foods, concentrated foods, natural foods, dried foods, and frozen foods.

For the advertiser who wants to stand out from all of this visual muddle, it's especially important to again follow advertising's prime rule—keep it simple. Crowded, fast-paced commercials with hard-to-understand messages just don't come across well on the screen in the few seconds of time allowed. A simply created, staged, and produced commercial will not only be more memorable; it can also help to keep costs in line with your budget.

The principles for creating a television commercial (also called a "spot") are the same as for any other form of advertising—a big sales idea with a strong benefit for the viewer. An easy formula to remember is this: (1) Name the product; (2) offer a benefit; (3) demonstrate how the product will deliver the benefit; (4) repeat the product name; and (5) ask for the viewer to act.

The most common lengths for television commercials are 10-, 30-, and 60-seconds. For the local advertiser, 30s are the most economical to produce, the easiest to purchase time for, and the most cost-effective. Research indicates that an average 30-second commercial is actually 75% to 92% as effective as a longer, more costly, 60-second spot. Ten-second commercials, referred to as I.D.'s (identifications), are usually cut-down versions of a longer commercial.

The backbone of any commercial is its structure—the form it will take. A strong, unified structure presented with imagination and believability will help the viewer follow and remember your message more easily.

The different structures used in television commercials are the following:

1. Demonstration: These prove an important point to the viewer about the product's benefit.

2. Stand-up Pitch (spokesperson): This is easy and inexpensive to produce. A word of caution, however: Select your spokesperson with care. When he or she leaves, a lot of goodwill you paid for goes too.

3. Testimonials: Real people who say honest, believable things about your product. Fake it and the viewer will know—immediately.

4. Dramatizations: Short, slice-of-life-stories that feature the product as the focal point. Use professional talent; amateurs usually aren't convincing enough.

5. *Humor:* This is tricky to do well. Unless your product is particularly suited to a humorous approach, don't even try it. People will generally laugh at the commercial and forget who is the advertiser.

6. *Problem Solution:* Present a problem and then offer a solution.

the television storyboard

The television storyboard, like the layout used in print media, is the blueprint of the commercial. The storyboard contains a series of drawings that indicate the main action taking place. Below each drawing is a written description of what is being pictured (video) and the actual words the viewer will hear (audio). Special sound effects and music are also described (see Figure 9–2).

A simple method to determine if your storyboard will come across well on the screen is to cover the words of the storyboard and just look at the pictures. Do the pictures alone convey the message? They should. Television is a visual medium; people tend to remember what they see more than what they hear.

producing the commercial

Preparing a television commercial that will stand out and be remembered is no do-it-yourself project. In other media there is a great deal an advertiser can do for himself; but for television he needs expert, professional help to guide him through the merry-go-round of producing a successful television commercial.

If you don't have an advertising agency, hire one, on a consulting basis, to produce your commercial; it'll be worth it. Advertising agencies normally work with film production companies who specialize in producing television commercials. In most cities, local television stations also will produce commercials for their advertisers.

When working with an ad agency, here's what happens. The agency representative will send copies of the client-approved storyboard to several film houses for bids, usually three. After the bids are received and a company to produce the commercial is selected, a pre-production meeting is arranged by the agency rep. It's an important meeting; the purpose is to review the commercial, frame by frame, and exchange ideas as to the best creative and technical way to produce it. This meeting normally includes the production company producer, TV director, writer,

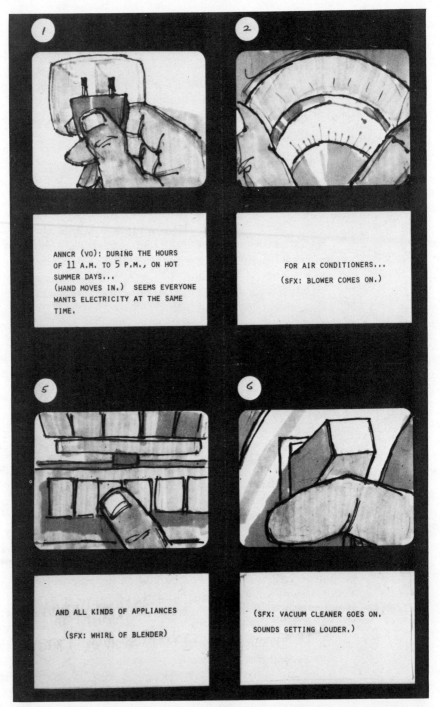

Fig. 9–2 Typical television storyboard. *Courtesy San Diego Gas & Electric Co.; Agency: Phillips-Ramsey, Inc.; Film Production: Cinira Commercials.*

126

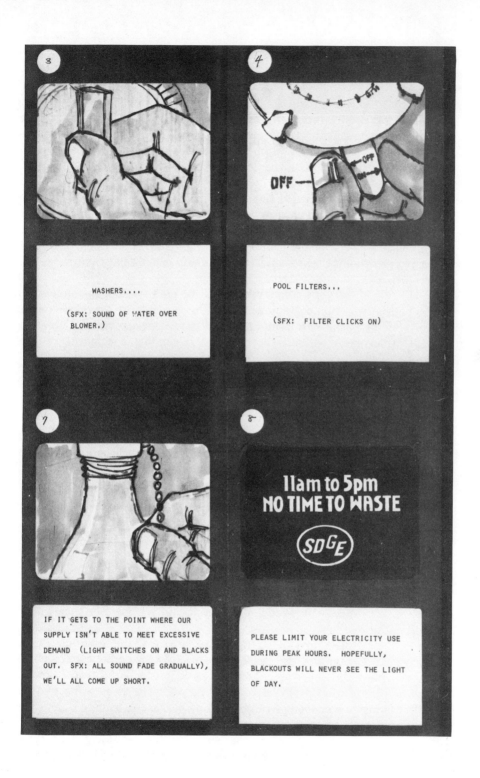

3

WASHERS....

(SFX: SOUND OF WATER OVER
BLOWER.)

4

OFF

POOL FILTERS...

(SFX: FILTER CLICKS ON)

7

IF IT GETS TO THE POINT WHERE OUR
SUPPLY ISN'T ABLE TO MEET EXCESSIVE
DEMAND (LIGHT SWITCHES ON AND BLACKS
OUT. SFX: ALL SOUND FADE GRADUALLY),
WE'LL ALL COME UP SHORT.

8

**11am to 5pm
NO TIME TO WASTE**

SDGE

PLEASE LIMIT YOUR ELECTRICITY USE
DURING PEAK HOURS. HOPEFULLY,
BLACKOUTS WILL NEVER SEE THE LIGHT
OF DAY.

art director, agency representative, and you, the client. At the meeting, a complete understanding and agreement should be reached on all details and costs relative to the commercial(s)—the selection of talent, sets, artwork, special effects, music, locations, and so on—and a shooting date should be scheduled.

Plan to attend the actual filming of the commerical; it's an experience you won't want to miss. The logistics involved in producing a simple 30-second commercial are unbelievable and have to be seen to be appreciated. Feel free to ask any questions or make suggestions, but direct them to your agency representative who, in turn, will relay them to the TV director.

Everyone concerned should be creative and resourceful to help keep production costs down whenever possible. A travel poster or color slide of Spain with flamenco music in the background can create a Latin atmosphere without the expense of sending a camera crew to Europe.

eighteen ways to improve your tv commercial

Be dull and routine in your commercial and the viewer will leap out of his or her chair and head for the kitchen or bathroom when it's on the air. But present an imaginative, believable, benefit-oriented commercial, and the viewer will reward you by looking and listening when it appears.

Here are some guidelines that will help you produce a more effective commercial:

1. Feature a single, benefit-oriented selling idea. Viewer recall decreases when multiple ideas are presented. Avoid confusing the viewer; use a minimal number of scenes and people (it's cheaper, too).

2. Make your selling idea easy to understand. Don't use fancy, complicated words or sentences.

3. Speak directly to the person to whom you are aiming your message. Although you are reaching thousands of people, communicate with the viewer on a one-to-one basis. In an ad for the *Wall Street Journal*, Reva Korda of Ogilvy & Mather stated, "I try to write an ad so it sounds as if I'm talking to somebody—talking to one person. A friend. Telling her what I want her to know about a product."

4. Hook the viewer right away. Don't spend time building suspense or curiosity; leave that approach to the "big boys" who can afford to

waste their money—you can't. Get the viewer involved in the first few seconds of the commercial. Don't wait; viewer interest drops rapidly. Keep your commercial strong from beginning to end. Have a definite beginning, middle, and ending—each step relating to the previous step. Don't let it fall down, particularly at the end.

5. Stay away from hard-to-believe superlatives; they tend to weaken your credibility. You don't believe exaggerated claims made by other advertisers, do you? Words can arouse, soothe, stimulate, or aggravate; use them to move the viewer to first believe—then act.

6. Use the same theme you are running in other media. If possible, use some of the same artwork and copy—it adds recall value to all of your advertising.

7. Mention your name at the beginning and at the end of the commercial—for those people who may have missed part of it. Use a title card or superimpose your name over the picture during the last few seconds.

8. Television is a visual medium—let the picture portion of the commercial tell the story. Use copy to reinforce the picture being shown. Don't show one subject and talk about another; picture and copy must relate, or you'll wind up confusing the viewer.

9. Test your commercial by reading it out loud. Do the words flow easily? In a 30-second commercial, there is time for about 60 words only. Will the announcer have to rush to get them all in? He or she shouldn't.

10. Once you have created the commercial, take the time to work out the details of producing it in advance. The storyboard and accompanying script should describe the scenes, props, action, sound effects, music, camera angles, and so on in detail. You can save hundreds of dollars—without sacrificing quality—at this stage of the game by being specific.

11. Use close-ups; keep distraction to a minimum and sets simple. Close-up shots are not only more dramatic, but they also reduce many of the costs of staging, sets, props, and talent. Hint at a particular setting with a few well-chosen props.

12. Demonstrate your product when possible. Show its unique features in a logical sequence—don't fake it. A word of caution about your demonstration: Consumer protection agencies will be all over your back if they feel it was false or misleading.

13. When selecting talent, choose average-looking men and women, similar to your neighbors. Your product is the star to be remembered, not some beautiful person. Get professional talent; amateurs usually look just that—amateurish.

14. Use videotape. With tape, you have the advantage of instant replay. If the commercial doesn't look right, you can make changes on the spot before the set is dismantled and the crew leaves.

15. Special effects can be interesting, but unless they are vital to the selling message, you're better off without them. Special effects are not only expensive to produce but they can be distracting; people will remember the effect and forget what you are selling.

16. Animation is fun to watch but does not rate high in believability with viewers. If you use animation, try it as a device to form your name—a logo or something that can be repeated many times to amortize its cost.

17. Before you agree to location shooting, be certain it's absolutely necessary. Taking a camera crew, actors, props, equipment, and so on out of the studio can become pretty expensive.

18. Leave entertainment to Hollywood. Many people mistakenly feel that to be successful, a television commercial has to be entertaining, but it ain't necessarily so. In fact, a commercial that is too entertaining can cause the viewer to forget what is being advertised.

How long should you run a commercial? That's easy: Run it as long as it's delivering *proven results*. Some successful television commercials have been running as long as five years.

And now, a word from our sponsor. . . .

10

MAIL ORDER AND DIRECT MAIL ADVERTISING

mail order—
bonanza or bankruptcy?

Each year thousands of new people enter the mail-order business, lured by promoters who claim anyone can "make profits in your spare time" with "little or no investment required" or who promise that "checks come rolling in." And, each year, just as many people leave the mail-order business disappointed, frustrated and with quite a bit less money than when they began. They learn, the hard way, that the mail-order business is no way to "get rich quick." Says David Ogilvy in *Confessions of an Advertising Man*, "The mail order advertiser has no retailers to shrink and expand inventories, to push his product or to hide it under the counter. He must rely on his advertisement to do the entire selling job." Yet mail-order advertising appears so deceptively simple that people jump into it without giving it much thought. They figure if they just run an ad, customers will be flooding the mail with checks for their products. If only it were that easy. The truth is that mail-order advertising is probably the most difficult and demanding form of advertising that exists.

Mail-order selling is a highly specialized method of selling a product directly to the consumer, through advertising and by mail, without the use of salespeople. In most cases, an ad persuades the prospects to order merchandise or inquire for further information; then direct mail is used to follow up and, hopefully, close the sale.

The mail-order entrepreneur wants and needs immediate tangible results—nothing less will do. Each advertisement produced has to more than pay for itself, and every mailing sent has to bring in dollars and cents results. Institutional and accumulative effect have little or no value to the mail-order advertiser.

In *Southwest Advertising & Marketing* magazine, Luther Brock, Ph.D., stated, ". . . There's no such thing as 'image creation' or 'institutional advertising' when it comes to making people part with their cash as a result of a mail-order pitch. Either the ad pulls or it doesn't. Either it pulls in the money—or else it's junked and a new one is tested."

Mail order is by no means a cheap way of producing sales. Profit margins on mail-order items have to be higher than on similar merchandise sold through other channels. The costs for ad and literature preparation, advertising space, purchasing and maintaining mailing lists, postage, and the like all have to be accurately determined and included in the price of the item being offered. The selling price should have a minimum profit spread of at least 4 to 1. For example, if an item costs $1 to produce, it should be sold for $4. In fact, some mail-order experts feel that a higher ratio of 5 to 1 would be more realistic.

132

To be successful in the mail-order business, you first must make sure your proposition is a good one. By that I mean you have to offer the customer something special: a unique product, unavailable anywhere else. The product should be such that it can create enough interest and desire to overcome the handicap of making a purchase by mail. If the item you're offering is weak, the best advertising campaign in the world won't sell it. You probably will fail.

the mailing list

The mailing list of prospects to whom the advertising will be directed is the next important part of the program. A successful mailing list is one that contains a large percentage of logical prospects for your product. If you were selling a golf shirt, for example, you should compile your list from golf club rosters, golf magazine subscribers or the members of golf associations.

Ready-made mailing lists are available from companies specializing in compiling them. They are gathered from directories, association membership rosters, subscription rolls, financial records, automobile registrations, birth records, homeowner lists, and other similar sources. Ready-made lists are offered for rent on a nonexclusive, one-time use basis. Most are on computers and are supposed to be 95% to 98% accurate. The cost of using a mailing list is figured on a per-thousand name basis and depends on how old the list is and how many times it has been used by other advertisers.

You can build your own mailing list from the names of present and past customers or respondents to previous mailings. When you put your list together, remember to:

1. Be certain the prospect is a logical, potential customer. Don't kid yourself about this.

2. Make sure all names and addresses are correct. Misspelled names can irritate people, and incorrect addresses waste your money.

3. Keep the list current; as many as 25% of the entries on an established mailing list can change in a single year; people move, die, retire, or make other changes in their status constantly.

4. Weed out duplicate names whenever it is practical to do so. But don't spend more money and time doing so than it is worth to you.

You can and should use the same mailing list as long as it is producing a profit. How do you know if the list is producing a profit? By constant testing, testing, and more testing.

test results

Testing the results of your sales efforts is not only important; it's vital. Without testing, you are literally playing a game of "blind man's bluff" by mail. Testing is a matter of keeping accurate records. It is time consuming and requires a great deal of attention to detail, but it must be done. In his book, *Scientific Advertising*, Claude Hopkins said, "Mail order advertising is traced down to the fraction of a penny." By testing the effect of your advertising, you will be able to determine if a new headline, a more convenient order form, or new lead-in paragraph to your sales letter will make a difference in the response. If one mailing does better than another, study it carefully. Try to find out why it was more effective so you can use what you learn in future mailings.

You can't guess at what will or will not work. You have to test and keep testing. One simple method for keeping track of ad response is by including a "key" in your address, a phrase such as "Dept. A-1" or "Dept. A-2," for example.

If you decide to go into the mail-order business, study every book on the subject. Find the "perfect something" to offer, latch onto a 14-carat mailing list, monitor results constantly, and maybe—just maybe—you might be lucky enough to "get rich quick."

twenty-seven ideas
for mail-order advertising

After years of study and trial and error, mail-order practitioners have developed guidelines that can increase response to mail-order advertising. You can benefit from their experience by following these basic rules:

1. Choose a product to sell that is unique and in demand—one that people need. It should be an item that is difficult to buy through retail outlets. The product should be of good quality; cheap or shoddy merchandise will kill any chance you may have for highly profitable repeat business and could get you in trouble with consumer protection agencies.

2. Develop a line of products that appeal to the same type of customer. You won't get rich on a single item.

3. Avoid handling low-priced merchandise; the mark-up is usually not enough to make a worthwhile profit for you.

4. Be prepared to substantiate any claims you make about the product. Many publications have a copy review board that approves all ads. Write for "Suggested Guidelines for Acceptance of Print Advertis-

ing," from the Direct-Mail Marketing Association, Inc., 6 East 43rd Street, New York, N.Y. 10017 for further information.

5. Be prepared to advertise on a continuous basis. Base your budget on the number of sales you need in order to have the ad at least pay for itself. You can start advertising by using small units of display space or classified advertising.

6. Ask for free editorial write-ups of your product(s) in the publications you advertise in (see Chapter 8).

7. Select media that are appropriate for your particular product. Study as many magazines as you can to determine which are the most suitable. Fishing lures obviously will sell better in sports rather than family magazines.

8. Experiment with different ad sizes, time periods, and copy appeals to find the right selling mixture for your product. The pulling power of one ad over another can vary by as much as 25 to 1.

9. Schedule your advertising for those months that have been proven to bring in results. For the Christmas market, advertise during September, October, and November; in your ad include the delivery time or "delivery before Christmas guaranteed." June, July, and August are normally weak periods for mail order.

10. Look for and use (if appropriate) publications that have special rates for mail-order advertisers, usually 10% to 40% less than their general rates.

11. Include a well-written sales letter. It is an indispensable part of any mailing and adds a much needed personal touch to the mailing effort. In a study of 100 successful ads, mail-order stateman John Caples reported the word "you" was used 31 times. It's a magic word; use it liberally in your letter.

12. Imprint the prospect's name and address in the salutation of the sales letter. It's worth the extra expense. If your mailing is too large, making it impractical for a personal salutation, substitute a bold typeset headline. Tests have shown that a headline does almost as well as a salutation.

13. Add a second color to the letter to underscore key phrases, sentences, or even entire paragraphs. It increases the pulling power.

14. Make it easy for the potential customer to respond; include a separate order form. If a check is to accompany the order, include a postage-paid reply envelope.

15. Print your mailer in two colors (one color plus black) rather than black alone. Studies indicate they generally produce better results than single-color mailers.

16. Reply cards, however, can be just as effective in one color as they are in two colors; save your money and print one-color reply cards.

⁜17. Use the new commemorative stamps on your first class envelopes; they attract extra attention. For bulk mailings, you can get special bulk rate, precanceled stamps—ask your postmaster.

⁜18. The best mailing list you can use is one developed from your inquiries and customers. If you have to rent a list, get one from an established mailing list broker. Restrict your mailing to real prospects; don't waste your money on unknowns.

⁜19. Put your own name on the mailing list. You'll learn just how long it takes your mailing to reach prospects and in what condition the mailing piece arrives.

20. Ask customers to pay by check; few will bounce. On C.O.D. orders, ask for a deposit, which will increase the number of paid orders. Avoid the phrase, "bill me"; it will limit your cash flow, and it's difficult to collect.

21. Adjust complaints quickly; remember that the customer is always right. Offer a money-back guarantee.

22. Keep an eye on shipping expenses. Offer to prepay postage on all orders that include payment. Figure the cost of the shipping in your selling price.

23. Calculate your break-even cost accurately by including all costs for the item itself, packaging, shipping, damage, refusals, and overhead.

24. Be prepared to ship merchandise within the time you state in your advertising. If you say you will "rush" an order in 10 days, you must ship it within that time. If no date for shipping is established, the customer has the right to expect it within 30 days. If you do not ship merchandise within the stated time or within 30 days the customer has the right to cancel the order.

25. Notify the customer if you can't ship in the stated time or within 30 days. Include a free means to reply (for example, a postage-paid postcard) with the notification. If the delay is to be more than 30 days, the customer must give consent.

26. Refund money quickly and cheerfully when an order is canceled and do it within seven days. A satisfied customer is your best bet for future sales.

27. Don't send unsolicited merchandise through the mail. It is illegal to pressure a customer for its return or to send a bill.

Once you have found the secret ingredients that make your ad pull like a slot-machine with diarrhea, run it until sales start falling off.

direct mail—
techniques to improve results

Over 4 billion dollars is spent by direct-mail advertisers each year, aimed at potential customers, promoting everything from inexpensive flower-seed packets to costly automobiles. These advertisers know that direct mail has some unique advantages compared to other media.

For example, with direct mail, you can do the following:

1. You can pinpoint your message to a specific market group. It goes directly to the customer. If you're selling business products, for instance, you can mail to local merchants and offices.

2. Your message doesn't have to compete with editorial copy or other advertising; it stands by itself.

3. You have greater flexibility in the design and format of the sales message. You are restricted only by your budget.

4. Response can be measured quickly and precisely. A telephone number, order form, or coupon provide ideal response mechanisms.

There are drawbacks, however. Some people seem to think that direct mail is a cheap medium for advertisers; it is not. The first-class postage alone for a mailing for 1,000 pieces in 1981 is $180. Add to that the expense of producing the mailing piece, compiling a list, printing the piece and envelopes, and inserting the material, and you come up with a higher cost per thousand than any other medium.

Does this mean you shouldn't use direct mail? No, but it does mean you should thoughtfully plan and carefully execute your next direct-mail program if you want it to pay off.

Advertising statesman Claude Hopkins said, "We learn the principles and prove them by repeated tests. This is done through keyed advertising, by traced returns, largely by the use of coupons. We compare one way with many others, backward and forward, and record the results. When one method invariably proves best, that method becomes a fixed principle." Test your mailing for results. Try a small sampling by sending two versions of the same piece to two different groups. Be sure, however, that the groups are similar in composition. Code your response cards to see which version pulls best for you. It's worth the extra effort.

A rule of thumb that many mail-order practitioners look for is a 3:1 ratio (three dollars in directly traceable income for every dollar spent on the mailing). When designing your mailing, there are many ways to keep your mailing costs down and still not compromise its effectiveness. Here are a few things you can do:

137

1. Use stuffers in your monthly statements being sent to present customers. Since you are already paying for the envelope and postage, a lightweight enclosure is an inexpensive way to announce upcoming sale events.

2. Use direct mail to bring in new sales from old customers. If they bought from you before, they're excellent prospects. If they haven't made purchases recently, try to find out why and win them back.

3. Use the "you" approach in your copy. Regard the customer as a friend. In a study on successful direct-mail copy, it was found that the most frequently used word was "you"; the second most successful word was "your." You should use "you" and "your" in your mailings. Get the idea?

4. Try a direct-mail newsletter; many people read them. Newsletters keep customers up to date on new product developments, sales features, industry news, and so on. You can sneak in a sales pitch, but be subtle.

5. Use a "teaser" on the envelope to get the prospect interested right away. Try something such as "Save 50% on - - - - - - -," or "Special Free Offer Inside."

6. Offer a free premium or bonus if the customer orders by a specific date. Get the customer to "act now!"

7. If your mailing is for a big-ticket item directed to high-income customers, spend the extra money necessary to give your mailing a first-class look. The piece should reflect the quality of the merchandise being offered.

8. Sell services as well as products. For example, if you're selling typewriters, offer a maintenance contract too.

9. Guarantee product satisfaction and return privileges. Make replacements or adjustments right away. Remember: The customer is always right.

10. Answer replies to bingo cards (reader-response cards in publications) or your own reply cards as soon as you receive them. Delay or forget to answer and you lose a potential sale.

11. "The more you tell, the more you sell" is an old advertising maxim that is worth remembering. Just be sure it is "you"-oriented. Go easy on gimmicks; give the reader solid information.

12. Include a one-page, one-side, sales letter in your mailings whenever possible. A good length is 250 to 350 words. Like all good copy, it should be written from the standpoint of the reader's interest in a language that is understandable and believable.

13. Make it easy for a prospect to order; include an order blank in

all your mailings. Remind the prospect to "order now, sign the enclosed card, and mail today; we pay postage." It's the call to action.

14. Remember to be "standard" in your mailings. Use standard-size paper for your mailing pieces. Odd-size sheets can be expensive. The same goes for envelopes—use a standard size. Odd-shaped envelopes may be attention getters, but they have to be custom made; the time and costs involved are high. And choose colors that can be printed with standard inks.

15. Plan to have several pieces grouped together and printed at the same time—in the same colors and on the same stock. It can reduce press time and, depending on how efficiently the pieces fit onto the press sheet, can save on paper costs.

16. Use colored paper. Printing on colored stock with a couple of colored inks can create the effect of a three-color job without the expense.

17. Don't use staples to fasten your mailers. Some readers refuse to open them. Staples tear paper, break fingernails, and irritate prospects. Self-mailers printed on heavy weight paper and tightly folded will travel and arrive in good condition.

18. Prepare an accurate paper dummy of your mailing for weighing purposes. Include all the pieces, even the paper clips. Be sure the weight comes within the postal limit. The smallest fraction of an ounce overweight can almost double your postage costs.

19. Plan ahead. Avoid rush jobs that have to be done on an overtime basis. If you do get into a rush situation, it's more economical to have the artist rush preparation of artwork than it is to have a printer go into overtime. Plan; plan ahead.

20. Watch your timing. Pre-season (prior to spring, summer, Christmas, etc.) is typically best for most retailers.

Direct-mail advertising is popular, and it can be effective. If you feel your advertising has been missing the mark lately, consider direct mail's rifle-shot approach. Review the above. Then get ready . . . aim . . . fire!

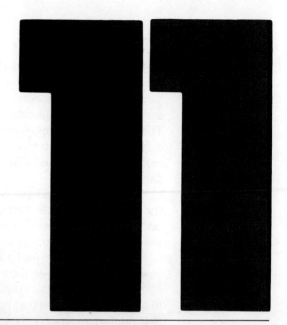

OTHER POPULAR ADVERTISING METHODS

yellow pages—
how to get those walking fingers
to stop at your ad

Through heavy promotion, Ma Bell has influenced people to use the Yellow Pages and let their "fingers do the walking." Because readers are ready to buy when they go through the Yellow Pages (nobody reads it for fun), it is a valuable medium for the local advertiser.

According to the results of an independent study done for the Pacific Telephone Company, 95% of the people interviewed found the Yellow Pages helpful in locating what they wanted; 78% said they contacted a firm after consulting the Yellow Pages, and half of these people made a purchase as a result.

The study further reported that the four most important factors in choosing a supplier (through the Yellow Pages) are (1) identification of brand names and trademarks, (2) amount of information in the ad, (3) location of the supplier, and (4) recognition of company name. Keep these four points in mind the next time you have to prepare an ad for the Yellow Pages.

Yellow Pages advertising space runs from a simple listing of name, address, and phone number to large display units. The latter offers the advertiser an opportunity to sell. All advertising is naturally placed in its own classification. If you're selling sportswear, your listing or ad will appear in the "Sportswear—Retail" section.

Rates for advertising space are quoted by the month. When a sales rep quotes you a price of "only $75," recognize it to mean "per month" and that it is actually an annual contract for $900.

As a business-telephone subscriber, you usually get one free listing in the Yellow Pages. If you want additional listings in other sections, you have to pay extra for them.

Some of the advertising options available are the following:

1. *Boldface listing*—the same as the free listing, but it's set in a heavy black type. You should consider boldface listings when you have to cross-reference a lot of products. For example, an office supply store might need to be included in the "office products," "stationery," and "typewriters" sections.

2. *Trademark listing*—features a manufacturer's trademark with a short selling message and a list of the distributors and dealers handling the product. The manufacturer may pay a proportionate share, and some allow the cost to be charged to a cooperative fund. Since many manufacturers run institutional advertising with the reminder, "to find the

141

dealer nearest you, look in the Yellow Pages," being included in a trademark listing could be of value to a dealer carrying the product.

3. *Display space*—sold in small- and large-size units, with room for descriptive copy and illustrations. Display ads normally appear on the same or adjoining pages of the regular listing. Position is determined by seniority; if you buy space each year, your ad will appear closer to the beginning of the section, whereas the newcomer is placed at the end.

Unlike other media that try to separate competitive ads, Yellow Pages ads are grouped together; you'll be surrounded by your competitors. For this reason, you should give your listing some very serious thought if you want those walking fingers to stop at your ad. Here are some tips that will be helpful:

1. List the product brands you carry (or service) and the selection of merchandise available.

2. If your firm offers repair services, be sure to identify the area(s) you serve.

3. Include information on whether orders can be placed by telephone.

4. List all major credit cards you accept.

5. Mention any special trade-in, budget plan, and the like that you offer.

6. Tie in your Yellow Page ad with other forms of your advertising. It can be done easily by asking people to "look us up in the Yellow Pages."

7. Experience is an important factor for customers and should be mentioned in your ad. Say something such as "handcrafted since 1928"; it helps establish your professionalism.

8. Include all the communities you serve. If possible, have a separate phone number for each or a toll-free number; make it easy for the prospective customer to reach you.

9. Use the same format (artwork, lettering, borders, etc.) that you use in your other forms of advertising for faster identification and added recall value.

10. Keep your copy tight and simple; write it as you would a telegram. Offer the reader a benefit; concentrate on the essentials and eliminate extraneous words. Avoid tricky phrases and don't exaggerate.

11. Use artwork for impact; spend extra for it. Remember that it

will represent you for a year. In addition, good-looking artwork helps establish an image of quality for your company.

12. Use bold lettering for emphasis, such as for the phone number, product, or service being offered. Don't overdo it.

13. Offer "all work guaranteed," but remember to be specific about what you guarantee. With new customers, it's an important consideration.

14. Include your store hours. If you're open evenings and weekends, be sure to say so. For customers with limited time to shop, this information is important.

15. If your store is hard to find, include a simple map so people can locate you easily.

16. Consider running your ad in surrounding directories. Suburban areas that are near can be a good source of potential customers.

One last reminder: Be sure to check your Yellow Pages advertising copy very carefully for errors or omissions. If a mistake slips by, you will have to live with it for a year.

outdoor advertising— big can be beautiful!

Long before television, before radio, and before magazines, posters dotted the country, advertising products of the day. They are still with us today as an advertising medium. Although posters—or billboards, as they are more commonly known—have become larger and more complex, their purpose remains the same: to reach the customer outside of the home.

Unlike newspaper, magazine, and television advertising, which are a combination of editorial plus advertising, outdoor is a total advertising medium. In some foreign countries, where other forms of media are limited or where illiteracy is high, outdoor is the dominant medium.

There are two basic categories of outdoor advertising: (1) posters (billboards) and (2) painted bulletins.

Billboards are referred to by their sheet size; either "24-sheet" (19 feet 6 inches × 8 feet 8 inches) or "30-sheet" (21 feet 7 inches × 9 feet 7 inches). Originally the term meant the amount of printed sheets needed to cover a board. Now, with larger printing presses, a board can be covered with as few as ten sheets; but the terms are still used. The 30-feet poster is the most popular size among national advertisers to sell brand-name products. Local advertisers rely on billboards to promote automotive-related supplies, sporting goods, fast-food outlets, travel accommodations, radio and TV stations, shopping centers, and the like.

Poster advertising space is sold by the "showing." A "100 showing" reflects complete coverage of an advertised area; a "50 showing" also indicates complete coverage of an area, but with less frequency. A showing may be purchased for only one month, but usually longer periods are contracted for at discounted rates. The advertiser is responsible for all costs in producing and shipping posters to the outdoor company. In most cases, at least 10% additional posters should be supplied for possible replacement use. A few contracts include the cost of producing the billboards as well as the space they will occupy.

Smaller posters (3-, 6-, and 8-sheet) called "Juniors" are popular with local advertisers, since they cost less and are easier to obtain than their bigger brother billboards. Junior posters are found mostly in localized shopping areas.

Painted bulletins are hand-painted, larger, and more elaborate than standard poster billboards. They are also more costly. Most are painted on sections and have some form of embellishment for dramatic effect, such as artwork extending beyond the limits of the board. Reproducing the advertiser's art and maintaining the sign in good condition is the responsibility of the outdoor company. Painted bulletins are contracted for individually, not by a showing. A "rotary" plan is generally available that allows the moving of a painted bulletin every 30 or 60 days to a different location. Because of the expense involved in producing a painted bulletin, the base contract period is for a minimum of one year.

Virtually all painted bulletins in urbanized areas are lighted to provide coverage of the heavy nighttime traffic. The poster panels employed in a showing are generally a combination of unilluminated and illuminated locations. The illuminated poster panels are located in those areas having sufficient nighttime traffic to warrant the extra expense. The ratio between unlighted and lighted poster panels varies from market to market.

Spectaculars are the Cadillacs of the business. They are the most expensive and elaborate of all outdoor signs. They are steel framed, and their construction can include all types of fancy lighting, animated objects, steam or smoke pouring forth, or even a real waterfall. They can truly be spectacular. Because of the obvious construction expenses involved, contracts are usually for extended periods.

In outdoor advertising, more so than in any other medium, it is important to follow advertising's number one concern—simplicity. The message must be easy to grasp by a person who only catches a glimpse of it while whizzing past. Here are some ideas that may help you attract this mobile reader:

1. Use one large photo or illustration. Big is not only beautiful, it is a necessity for maximum attention and impact. Crop close for dramatic effect. For instance, if you are advertising sunglasses, get in close to the eyes. Figures of people should be silhouetted; backgrounds normally interfere with legibility.

2. Limit your copy to only a few words—between six and ten maximum. The words you select should be short and instantly readable.

3. Coordinate artwork with copy. Volkswagen's famous "Mass Transit" poster showing a group of nuns boarding a VW bus is an excellent example of how a few well-chosen words and the right artwork can be combined to effectively convey an idea that is understood easily and quickly.

4. Select bold, easy-to-read type for your message. Thin or fancy lettering is difficult to read from a distance.

5. Be bright in your use of colors; avoid soft pastel shades. Use primary colors (red, yellow, blue) and black over large areas. Get good contrast between the letters and background so they stand out; black and yellow is a good combination.

6. Identify your product or service distinctly.

7. Give brief but clear directions to your location, when appropriate, for the tired traveler who is looking for a good place to stay, visit, or eat; a few words such as "ahead one mile," or "turn right at next intersection" can make the difference.

Layouts and finished artwork for outdoor advertising are not made to full poster size. How would you ever get a proof into a client's office for approval? Layouts are typically drawn to a scale of 2¼ to 1, or 13½ × 6 inches (for a 24-sheet poster.) When a smaller layout size is desired, 10⅛ × 4½ inches is acceptable. However, for finished (camera-ready) artwork, the preferred size is 27 × 12 inches or 36 × 16 inches.

Always remember, with outdoor advertising, to keep your message simple by making it big, bold, and brief.

advertising specialties— gifts that keep on giving

If you've ever been given a ballpoint pen with an advertiser's name printed on it, you have been the recipient of an "advertising specialty." An advertising specialty is any useful item imprinted with the giver's name, logo, address, and, frequently, a brief slogan or advertising message.

The advertising specialty business started fifty years ago, in Iowa, when housewives were given, free, a combination matchbox holder and match dispenser bearing the advertiser's name and address. Then along came calendars with the name and address of a local feed store or its equivalent. But the really big boom began after World War II, when the ballpoint pen was developed. Since then, imprinted ballpoint pens have been given away freely by advertisers, like confetti at a political convention. And today, an estimated one billion dollars is spent on more than 10,000 different advertising specialty items each year. It's big business.

Advertising specialty items are given free, without obligation, to prospects and customers. They are used by advertisers to create goodwill for their company, attract new prospects, introduce a new product or service, or for use as a door opener for salespeople.

There are three categories of advertising specialty products:

Inexpensive Objects: Costing only a few cents, such as ballpoint pens, rulers, matchbooks, key tags, litter bags, nail clippers, and yardsticks.

Calendars: One of the oldest and probably most often used items. It would be difficult to find a home or place of business that does not have at least one imprinted calendar.

Executive Gifts: For selected individuals at the management level of an organization. Higher in cost than other items, they are typically in the form of attaché cases, desk sets, luggage, silver trays, desk clocks, or radios.

As an advertising medium, specialty items offer their own unique advantages. First, they are welcomed by customers, who happily accept them since they are free. Second, the right item has a long advertising life. Calendars are a good example; they have a life span of twelve months. How many other advertising media can make that claim? And third, the unit cost is low when you consider the exposure value of the message—it is continually exposed to the recipient and other people.

The industry is divided into three classifications:

1. The *Supplier*, who manufactures the item and makes it available for sale to advertisers through advertising specialty distributors.

2. The *Advertising Specialty Distributor* who, in addition to providing the item, offers counseling, ideas, art and copy service. The distributor receives a commission from the supplier for the order placed; there is no charge to the customer for his or her service.

3. The *Direct Selling House,* a combination of supplier and distributor. It manufactures its own products and, through its own sales force, sells them directly to an advertiser.

The largest percentage of the advertising specialty business is generated from September to November for delivery before Christmas and New Year's. Normal delivery time is 30 days; during the busy season, it's about six weeks.

It's fairly easy to get your advertising message imprinted on an item. First, decide to whom you will be giving it and what type of item would be practical. (Imprinting can be done on almost any size metal, wood, plastic, paper, cloth or glass product.) Then call in a local advertising specialty distributor. You can locate a distributor in the Yellow Pages of your telephone book under "Advertising Specialties." Tell the distributor what you have in mind and ask to have catalogs and samples brought to your office (there is normally no charge for this service) for evaluation.

There are also some things to consider when selecting an advertising specialty item:

1. Select something people need and would find useful. For instance, a low-cost item for an airline could be a luggage tag—the traveler would find it helpful in identifying his or her luggage. A key chain would be a natural giveaway for automobile dealers.

2. Choose a good product of acceptable quality. Remember that it will carry your company name and represent you for a long time.

3. Limit distribution to those customers and prospects who warrant the expense—think in terms of specific groups you are trying to reach.

Because the cost depends both on the item you select and the quantity purchased, select an appropriate product in a quantity to fit your budget. The price quoted should include all costs, including delivery.

The distributor will use your artwork (or will have artwork prepared for an additional fee) and arrange for imprinting and delivery.

Measuring the effectiveness of specialty items as an advertising medium is difficult, if not nearly impossible. If knowing results is important to you, you'd better pass up using specialties. But if you would like to create some goodwill, attract new prospects, introduce a new product, or just say "thank you" to customers, a specialty item is a good idea with a lasting effect.

put more sell in your sales

He who whispers down a well
About the goods he has to sell
Will never reap the golden dollars
Like him who shows them round and hollers

ANONYMOUS

It is surprising how many advertisers go through all the usual gymnastics of running a special "sale" promotion only to stick their heads down a well and whisper. A sales promotion is definitely not the time to whisper.

The difference between a sale that fails and one that succeeds is usually a matter of using what is already there. Important details make the difference between a whisper and a holler.

If your recent "sales" have been less than what you expected, you might consider some of the following suggestions to help put yell into your sell.

1. Plan ahead. You've heard that before, but a successful sales promotion is dependent on many factors—pricing, merchandise, availability, timing, advertising, and so on. This all takes time, planning, and coordination. Allow sufficient time before the event so that displays, ads, mailers, commercials, and the like can be created, produced, and delivered on time. Last-minute thinking causes errors and missed opportunities.

2. Don't let the theme of the event override the fact that you are having a real "honest-to-goodness," "come and get 'em" sale. "Sale" is the star of the promotion and should dominate your efforts.

3. Keep your ad layouts simple and organized so that the potential customer can easily and quickly find items of interest. It should look visually exciting, but not cluttered.

4. Copy should use proven sell words, such as "announcing," "just arrived," "it's here," "sensational," "remarkable," "compare," "bargain," "hurry!", and "last chance." Include information a customer needs to make a buying decision—colors, fabrics, sizes, selection, and so on. List store hours, dates of the sale, and different credit cards accepted. Don't

forget locations and phone numbers of all participating stores. Avoid institutional copy. Sell; don't serenade your customer.

5. Coordinate all media—newspapers, radio, television, mail, and so on—for maximum impact and efficiency. Make sure they all carry the same unmistakable message and theme: "We're having a sale."

6. Send an advance notice to current customers in your monthly mailings and statements. They are especially good prospects and will appreciate the special treatment. The cost will be low since you are paying for the addressed envelope and postage already. If your firm uses a postage meter, arrange to have a "Sale now going on" message put on the indicia. Let the recipient know you are having a sale even before the envelope is opened.

7. Be sure everyone in your organization is briefed on the coming event and understands the part he or she will play in its success. Provide them with as much information as possible—dates, merchandise reductions, and the like. Don't forget your telephone people. They should be prepared to answer all possible customer inquiries. Copies of sale ads posted at employee stations make for fast, easy reference.

8. Inside the store(s), bombard customers with reminders. Use sale banners, streamers, posters, displays, price tags, and so on. Create a colorful and exciting event. Strategically and prominently display sale merchandise so customers will have to pass other related items to get to the advertised specials.

9. Tie in with manufacturers, when possible, for in-store sampling and demonstrations. Some manufacturers supply audio-visual equipment. If it fits your needs, grab it.

10. Insert sale flyers in all packages of merchandise sold just prior to and during the sale period. The cost is minimal, and the effort can produce unexpected results. Consider featuring "unadvertised" items.

11. If possible, offer special "early shopping hours" and/or "moonlight shopping hours" for working people and senior citizens. Feature special sale items that will appeal to these groups.

12. Have brightly colored, removable signs made and attached to the sides of company trucks and vans. They become, in effect, moving billboards announcing the sale wherever they go.

13. Invite copy and art people to participate in the sale. They'll get valuable first-hand experience of the results of their efforts. Afterwards, have them evaluate results and propose changes that will improve your next promotion.

14. Don't forget to arrange for additional sales clerks to be on hand for large volume promotions. All the advertising in the world cannot bring back a lost sale because a customer couldn't get service.

Holler, don't whisper. By proper planning and coordination, your "sale" promotion will be heard all over town.

sales promotions can promote sales

Advertise, or the chances are the sheriff will do it for you.
PHINEAS TAYLOR (P.T.) BARNUM (1810–1891)

P.T. Barnum was not only a great showman, he was a master of sales promotion as well. His genius for spectacular promotions made such personalities as General Tom Thumb (a dwarf) and Jenny Lind (a Swedish singer) world famous. Barnum's success was due not only to his widely exaggerated claims, which were often misleading, but in large measure to his effective use of newspaper advertising, handbills, posters, parades, and street exhibitions.

The *Ayer Glossary of Advertising and Related Terms* defines promotion as, "Any effort or activity designed to encourage the acceptance or sale of a product or service." Viewed another way, Eugene Mahany, in *Advertising Age* magazine, explained, "The difference between brand-sell advertising and promotional advertising can be expressed . . . brand-sell advertising tells consumers why they should buy a product; promotional advertising tells consumers why they should buy a product now."

A sales promotion is used in conjunction with advertising to (1) inform, persuade, and remind customers of a company's products or services; (2) reinforce a company's business image for quality, leadership, low prices, and so on; (3) increase a company's share of the market; (4) attract new customers and retain old ones; (5) introduce new products or services; (6) create goodwill with its public.

By coordinating promotional activities with advertising and personal selling, an advertiser can increase store traffic, resulting in greater sales throughout the entire store. A survey conducted by the Newspaper Advertising Bureau revealed that "each dollar spent on advertising sales items resulted in another dollar being spent by customers on something else in the store."

A promotional effort should center around a central theme, general merchandise, or a specific product. It is built on a solid selling concept, such as a special sales event, an unusual price discount, a contest, or a special premium offer. Most promotions take the form of clearance sales, birthday sales, dollar days, penny days, holiday sales, sidewalk sales, midnight sales, or you-name-it sales.

Here are some original promotional events that have been used and from which you might get some ideas:

1. A Tootsie Roll Sweepstake featured an automobile filled with Tootsie Roll candies. People were invited to guess how many of the candies were in the car. The correct guess won the car; other prizes were also awarded.

2. A California shopping center had a "Wheel of Fortune" set up in their mall. Shoppers had the opportunity to win back their purchase price—up to $100 in merchandise certificates—by matching the store name on their purchase receipt with the store name spun on the wheel.

3. In Moline, Illinois, a clothing store had an Ugly Tie Contest. In exchange for any ugly tie, $1.00 was deducted from the retail price of a new tie in stock.

4. A department store in Philadelphia celebrated its anniversary with Beat-the-Clock discounts. From the store's opening until 12:00 noon, prices were marked down on a variety of outstanding merchandise. At 12:01, any Beat-the-Clock tagged merchandise still remaining returned to its original retail price.

5. A clothing store in Ohio advertised a Blue Jean Trade-In. Customers bringing in old blue jeans were allowed $3 toward the price of a new pair.

6. A bank in Illinois deposited a ton of coffee in their vault. A free 2-pound can of coffee was given to anyone opening a savings account or depositing $100 or more in an established account.

7. A chain of sound equipment stores in Chicago offered free T-shirts, emblazoned with an advertising message on the front and back, to customers making a purchase of $10 or more.

8. In Wichita, Kansas, Gary Layton impersonated famous people over a discount store's loudspeaker system. His most popular impressions featured John Wayne asking customers to buy a bird bath, Henry Fonda selling flower pots, Cary Grant touting Easter lilies, and Gregory Peck advertising garden hoses. Customers flocked to the patio-garden department, hoping to connect the familiar voice with a face.

9. A Japanese restaurant chain had patrons checking their chopsticks for prizes. Customers who uncovered colored tips on their chopsticks received two free movie tickets.

10. In Utah, a department store delivered one dozen free roses

to mother, on Mother's Day, if a son or daughter purchased a 3-piece outfit as a Mother's Day gift.

11. A chain of Chicago hardware stores promoted kerosene lamps after one of New York's massive blackouts. "It can happen in Chicago" was the display theme. The lamps were renamed "brownout lights."

If you want to go the contest route, be sure to check with your lawyer. Contests and sweepstakes are subject to federal and state laws, so you have to be careful.

Once you have decided on a theme, you can use some or all of the following sales promotion techniques:

1. Window displays—provocative and attractive enough to make the passersby notice the displayed merchandise and convince them to enter the store.

2. Interior displays—set up to help the customers locate the advertised merchandise, make a decision to buy, and serve themselves.

3. Sales literature and handouts—to interest customers and draw their attention to the special feature(s) of the product(s).

4. Point-of-purchase displays—to capture the customers' attention and encourage impulse purchases.

5. Specialty items—such as calendars, balloons, pens, pencils, novelties, and free samples—for use as give-aways.

A good promotion can bring customers into the store, but it can't fully succeed without the help of well-informed salespeople. Tibor Taraba, noted ad personage, said, "When salespeople have been involved in sales promotions from the very beginning, they're always more enthusiastic about it and they use it more effectively." Salespeople should be briefed in advance about the promotion and the products being advertised. The best-planned promotion will be for naught if your sales staff isn't prepared. Telephone answering personnel should also be aware of what is happening so they can answer questions and assist customers who phone for information.

Putting together a successful sales promotion requires a lot of merchandising know-how, some advertising skills, a bit of daring, and a tremendous amount of imagination. Make it exciting and fun—for your customers and yourself. Create excitement for your promotion and parade it before the public with all the hoopla you can generate. I challenge you to

"Step right up, ladeez an' gennulmen, and put on the most colossal, the most stupendous, the most fabulous promotion show on earth."

contests, self-liquidators, premiums, rebates, and sampling

It was 1851 when B. T. Babbitt first offered customers the opportunity to exchange coupons packed in soap packages for a series of decorative color prints. Since then, advertisers have improvised on and expanded this concept of promoting sales by offering their customers some kind of incentive to purchase and use a product. Today, for example, it's easy to find a fast-food chain where you can "Buy a Coke and keep the glass."

There are many types of sales promotional efforts and just as many definitions. Simply stated, sales promotions are those activities between a manufacturer and a dealer for the purpose of stimulating sales.

Sales promotions made directly to the ultimate consumer by a manufacturer are designed to presell and induce immediate sales of a product. Most techniques force the customer to try, or at least examine, a new or established product and hopefully continue its use long after the promo ends.

When customers respond to a promotion in great numbers, the dealer is encouraged to carry the item and prominently display it. The dealer knows it will sell faster than a similar product that doesn't have the benefit of a promotional hype. This positive action on the dealer's part is one reason why national manufacturers establish large budgets for their sales promotion ventures. In one year, Nestle's spent $5.3 million in advertising and redemptions just to give away a free package of their new cookie mix to housewives.

There are many forms of sales promotions. Some of the most common are contests and sweepstakes, self-liquidators, premiums, rebates, and samplings. Let's take a look at these and see how they were implemented by different advertisers.

Contests and Sweepstakes: Contests and sweepstakes are two of the most popular approaches. Even though the odds of winning are often astronomical, people still dream of winning a free trip to some faraway place, or a new car, or an expensive fur coat, just for writing why they should be the lucky winner ". . . in twenty-five words or less."

1. Avis Rent-A-Car gave away five new Plymouth Volares during their "Win-A-Car" sweepstakes; all a person had to do to be eligible was send in his or her name and address on a 3 × 5 inch card. That was it.

2. Ralston Purina offered pet owners a chance to "Win your dog's weight in gold" for simply writing why they felt their canine was worth the prize.

3. Somerset Importers promised a "World Tour" to the winner of their contest for answering three questions correctly. The answers were to be found on labels of their Johnnie Walker bottles.

4. Coca-Cola appealed to young people by offering a custom designed van, nicknamed a "Deninmachine." Details were packed in Coke cartons.

Self-liquidators: A self-liquidator is a low-priced or unique item, unavailable elsewhere, usually requiring proof-of-purchase evidence and an additional cash outlay.

1. Phillip Morris promoted an attractive "You've come a long way, baby" sweater for only $9 plus the bottoms from two packs of Virginia Slims cigarettes.

2. Marlboro sold over 30,000 pieces of western-related gear, valued at over half a million dollars, through their Country Store Catalog.

3. Scott Paper Company advertised digital watches for only $29.95 and five proofs-of-purchase of their Viva paper towels.

4. International Harvester didn't need proof-of-purchase when they offered a Coleman sleeping bag to anyone who took a test ride in one of their Scout vehicles, plus $8 in cash.

5. Kool cigarettes thinks big. They promoted a 12-foot-long Hobie catamaran (delivered to the dealer nearest you) for $699 and the end panel from one of their cartons.

Premiums: You know that you don't get something for nothing, but some premiums come pretty close to it. The premium is free, but a product purchase is usually necessary.

1. Dixie Cups gave away a "Free Westclox Alarm Clock" to anyone who sent in seven box tops.

2. 9-Lives Cat Food gave cat lovers a "Morris the Cat" T-Shirt in exchange for 30 of their labels.

3. General Motors hoped to offset sluggish sales by advertising, "Buy a new Opel and get 200 gallons of gas, absolutely free."

Rebates: Once used only by the food industry, rebates have become extremely popular with manufacturers who refund part of the purchase price on items ranging from small accessories to cars.

1. Del Monte advertised, "Five Del Monte labels will get you $1.00" during one of their promos.

2. Jockey Underwear sent buyers, with proof-of-purchase, a check for $3.00.

3. Porsche Audi Dealers offered an immediate rebate with a "no strings attached" of $1,000 off the sticker price of any new Audi 100 LS.

Sampling: A sample is a smaller size package of a product that is usually accompanied by a coupon the recipient can apply toward the purchase of a full size package. Samples are distributed to the public at supermarkets, to their door, through the mail, or attached to special advertisements.

1. Excedrin ran an ad with a coupon good for one free "12-tablet sample bottle" of their headache remedy.

2. McCormick/Schilling actually had free samples of their Spaghetti Sauce Mix and Season-All packages inserted in major Sunday newspapers. Expensive—but who could resist keeping the sample.

Don't let the lack of a large budget discourage you from trying something. My first sales promotion effort was a "Draw Felix the Cat" contest with prizes such as bicycles, paint sets, and assorted toys that were donated in exchange for mention in the ads. This relatively low-budget effort breathed new life into a product that was on the verge of being discontinued.

Now, in twenty-five words or more, write a plan for a sales promotion that can create some excitement in your own advertising program. You can be a lucky winner, too.

coupons offer redeemable features

Half the money I spend on advertising is wasted, and the trouble is I don't know which half.

JOHN WANAMAKER (1838–1922)
Merchant and Philanthropist

Mr. Wanamaker is typical of many of us in advertising today. We run ads without ever really knowing if we are getting our money's worth. We know we should be doing some sort of testing to determine which ads are worth the investment and which ads are just bombing out, but we never seem to get around to it. The procedure's too expensive, too complex and difficult to monitor, or we're just too busy with other things. If you fit into one of these categories, you might try coupons.

Keeping track of coupon advertising response is easy. All you have to do is count the coupons as they come in. Nothing could be simpler. If you want pinpoint accuracy, you can key the coupon. When it runs in different media, just insert a small code like "LAT312" (*Los Angeles Times*, March 12th) within the coupon.

In addition to being useful to test results, coupons have proven to have good pulling power. You may use a coupon within your ad, or your entire ad can be a coupon. For example, if you want to entice the reader to come into your store, an ad featuring 10% off several different items is one way of turning your entire ad into a coupon. Physically counting coupons is one way of checking ad response; there have also been studies that show the positive effectiveness of coupon ads. Gaines Burger Dog Food ran two advertisements for their cheese-flavored Gaines Burgers. Both ads were full page, in color, in the same magazine, and featured a young boy with his dog. The only difference was that one features a "Save 15¢" store coupon; the other didn't. Here's how they compared when they were tested for effectiveness:

	WITH COUPON	WITHOUT COUPON
Noted ad	57%	40%
Saw ad and associated	40%	28%
Read most of ad	12%	2%

Coupons can also help if you have store location problems, or if you just want to generate more in-store traffic. Nestle offered a "Free, one package of new Nestle's Cookie Mix (93¢ value)" just for bringing the coupon into the store. It was a combination coupon/sampling program promotion that was a big traffic builder. Speaking of in-store traffic, a Macy's Department Store survey several years ago revealed that 38% of the shoppers who specifically came to see and perhaps buy an advertised item purchased an average of 5.75% additional products, whether or not they purchased the advertised item.

Coupons are a favorite of a million packaged goods manufacturers who distributed eight billion coupons in 1978. These coupons were designed to promote product trial and convert the trier into a regular user, reach large numbers of prospects more economically, encourage the use of large size items, and increase trade buy-ins.

Coupons come in many forms. Here are some of the more popular:

Newspaper Coupon: Sunshine Crackers offered a "50¢ Off" store coupon toward a cheese purchase for two proofs-of-purchase from a Sunshine Krispy or Hi-Ho Crackers box. John Deere advertised a group of coupons worth a whopping "$380 Off" for their snowmobiles and related accessories.

In-pack Coupon: Inside specially marked boxes of Kleenex tissues was packed a coupon worth 10¢ toward the purchase of Orange Juice from Florida. They even tied in an "Extra Cold Fighters Bonus" offer of a clinical oral thermometer for only $1.

On-pack Coupon: Kellogg's had two coupons on one of their Raisin Bran cereal boxes. One was worth "10¢ Off" the next purchase of Kellogg's Frosted Rice; the other was worth "7¢ Off" the next purchase of Kellogg's Raisin Bran. On the same box, they also offered a "25-piece School Pencil Box" for $1.95 plus two proof-of-purchase seals.

Tie-in Coupon: Diet-Rite teamd with L'Eggs Hosiery and offered to send women a coupon worth $1 on any package of L'Eggs hosiery in return for 12 cap liners from Diet-Rite Cola bottles.

Refund Coupon: Dow Chemical sent refund checks worth up to $5.45 in exchange for proofs-of-purchase of their Saran Wrap, Ziploc Bags, Oven Cleaner, and Bathroom Cleaner.

In-store Coupon: A clothing store gave "$1 off coupons" to everyone who bought something. The coupons were good toward future purchases.

Coupons are distributed in newspapers, Sunday supplements, magazines, as free-standing inserts, in or on packages, through the mail, or in your store. Newspapers carry most of the coupons advertised, but they also have a low redemption rate (approximately 2%). In- or on-pack coupons seem to do the best (20% redemption rate), with direct mail running a healthy second (13.3%).

Using direct mail, advertisers can control the costs, timing, and distribution of coupons. As a retailer, you may have customer credit systems; or if you accept orders by phone or mail, you automatically have excellent mailing lists of prospects. You can include coupons in your monthly statements, saving postage and envelope costs. Local noncompetitive advertisers, especially those located in shopping centers, may find it practical and economical to share in a joint coupon mailing effort by combining individual coupons into one mailing package.

Coupon promotions can take many forms. Perhaps you can adapt some of these ideas for your use:

1. Jewelry Items—"Free Engraving" coupon good on any jewelry purchase over $XX.

2. Leather Goods—"Free Gold-Stamped Initials" coupon on any purchase over $XX, or a "25% Off" coupon good on one suitcase when purchased at the same time as another of higher value, at the full price.

3. Sports Equipment—"One Free Pair of Socks" coupon with every pair of jogging shoes purchased of $XX value.

4. Office Products—Coupon good for "One Free Ream of Typing Paper" with the purchase of any typewriter of more than $XX value. Or a "Free Desk Set" with every purchase of a new desk of $XX value.

5. Restaurants—Coupon good for "One Free Dinner" when a second dinner of equal or greater value is purchased.

6. Services—A coupon good for "One Month's Free Pool Cleaning Service" with a XX year(s) pool cleaning contract.

As you can see by these various ideas, coupon offers are only limited by your imagination. A word of caution about using coupons, however: Don't forget to do the following:

1. Explain clearly what the coupon offers. If it is a $1 off deal, be sure to specify if the coupon applies to all merchandise, just to regularly priced items, or just to specific articles.

2. Identify items by brand name, quantity, price, size, and model number(s) if possible.

3. Set a limit on how many can be used—usually, one per customer.

4. Include an expiration date.

Be innovative in your coupon advertising. Offer something of value, something appealing, a bargain to your prospective customers. You don't want to waste your advertising money, and today's consumers want to get their money's worth. Try coupons, with their redeemable features.

PUBLICITY

ten newsworthy events
to hang a hook on

I get more advertising space without paying for it than anyone in the country.

HARRY HOUDINI (1874–1926)

Harry Houdini will always be remembered by the public for his daring feats of escape and his incredible magical prowess. Yet we in advertising would do well to also remember him for his highly imaginative promotional skills. He never missed a chance to publicize himself. When he was performing in a theater, he used window displays—of handcuffs, manacles, and leg irons from which he had freed himself—to attract and lure the public inside. Handbills announcing his daring exploits were printed and widely distributed in advance of his appearances. To help sell tickets to his stage performances, Houdini performed some of his most sensational stunts in public for free, with a great deal of fanfare, which resulted in large amounts of free publicity and ticket sales.

Am I suggesting you attempt to get out of a strait jacket while hanging by your ankles 75 feet above the ground in order to promote your business? Hardly, but I am suggesting you take a lesson from this remarkable man and do what he did—use plenty of imagination to publicize your company activities.

Publicity is a free form of advertising that anyone can obtain simply by sending prepared, newsworthy information to newspapers, radio, and television stations (Figure 12–1). An event doesn't have to be as spectacular as one of Houdini's stunts to be accepted by editors, but it must have news value. Announcements of new products, important management changes, and other notable company happenings are of interest to editors and their readers.

Much of the time such events don't just happen, they are planned (notice I said, "planned," not manufactured) by an alert, publicity-minded person within a company. He or she continually seeks and finds those newsworthy elements in what a company does, then writes them up and sends them to the news media.

Some company events that usually go unnoticed but are good hooks to hang a publicity release on are the following:

1. Retail store openings and ground-breaking and ribbon-cutting ceremonies. Invite a prominent personality to share the spotlight for added news value.

SUBJECT:	"Advertising Basics," new book
CONTACT:	Janet Lawrence (714) 555-1234

FOR IMMEDIATE RELEASE:

"Advertising Basics," by Hal Betancourt, a comprehensive book which can serve as both a working tool and a reference source for advertising people, has been published by the Spectrum Division of Prentice-Hall.

The book contains specific, down-to-earth advice and information on advertising agencies, ad budgeting, production, media (newspapers, magazines, radio, television, direct mail), a glossary and other advertising subjects.

There is easy-to-understand data on: measuring ad space and calculating rates; how to get free publicity; "A.I.D.A.," a simple formula for writing an ad; how to stay out of legal hot water; and even how to get those walking fingers to stop at a Yellow Page ad.

Helpful tips and useful suggestions are liberally scattered throughout the illustrated book.

"Advertising Basics" is available, in softcover, through local bookstores or wherever business books are sold.

Fig. 12–1 Typical news release form.

2. Store anniversaries. If the store is older than ten years, be sure to include a photo; vintage photos are popular.

3. Appointment of new store owners, managers, or personnel. Keep it on the executive level.

4. National sales awards to store owners, managers, and personnel.

5. Store remodeling or enlargement plans. Include information on how many new people will be employed, new product lines added, sales anticipated, and the like.

6. New car announcements by automotive dealers.

7. National, regional, or district association meetings attended by company personnel.

8. Sales volume figures, earnings, and dividend announcements at appropriate times of the year for the business pages.

9. Store sponsorship of workshops or instructional classes for the benefit of their customers. Include dates and a schedule of topics.

10. Charitable donations. Don't mail the check. Have a photo taken of the presentation for publicity purposes; it will profit both the charity and the donor.

Here are a few examples of how to begin a news release. Notice how the news "hook" allows a company to logically and subtly include its name:

1. "Beaded pants for men are the new fashion trend, according to John B. Smith, president of the ABC Clothing Store, who just returned to town after viewing the new fall collection in . . ."

2. "Louise Brown, manager of ABC Department Stores, has been appointed Regional Director of the Retailer's Association . . ."

3. "Ground-breaking ceremonies are planned for the new 50,000 square feet ABC Hardware Store to be located in . . ."

4. "Frank L. Fish, sales manager for ABC Discount Stores, has been honored for his successful efforts in . . ."

Some of the items I have mentioned are so common to most companies that they are largely ignored. That's okay; let the others, like your competitors, ignore them. You, however, follow Houdini's lead; it will work like magic for you.

how to submit new product publicity

Have you ever noticed the "New Products" section in your favorite magazine? Most publications have one. This section usually contains a variety of newly developed products of interest to the magazine's readers.

Many businesspeople don't realize these write-ups are run free as editorial matter by the magazine. And because they are editorial matter, readers respond to them, sometimes more so than to a paid advertisement.

Editors fill these columns with information they receive from individual companies, advertising agencies, or public relations firms.

Unfortunately, many worthwhile new product announcements are not sent to magazines because no one in the company "knew it was possible," "had the time," or "knew how to go about it." What a waste!

It's a fairly simple procedure to submit material for editorial consideration. Here's all you have to do:

1. Write a news release that contains detailed, accurate information about your product. The news release can be typed on your company letterhead. It should be double-spaced, with at least one-inch margins on both sides of the paper. Quality, not quantity, is what an editor is looking for, so don't make the release more than one page (one side) in length.

2. At the top of the page, include the subject of the release and the name and phone number of a person the editor can contact for information. Make sure the most important information is at the beginning of the release, with lesser information trailing at the end. This makes it easy for an editor to cut the material from the bottom upward, to fill space, and to still retain the main features of the item. Don't write the headline; editors reserve this privilege for themselves.

3. If you remember to answer the news reporter's standard questions—Who?, What?, Where?, When?, and How?—you should end up with a pretty acceptable piece.

4. Never, never make the mistake of having the news release sound like an advertisement for your product. Editors can spot "sell" copy very quickly and, with the same speed, will toss your tender offering into the trash can.

5. Include a black-and-white photograph of the product (4 × 5 inches, 5 × 7 inches, or 8 × 10 inches). It should be of professional caliber; Polaroids and amateur snapshots won't cut the mustard. Get a pro to take the photo. The investment will be worth it. If the product size is important, include a photo or drawing of a hand or a person or some device that will give the reader an idea of its proportions. Include your company name in the photo, but be subtle. Try to show it on the product itself or in the background. Don't be obvious; it could be resented by the editor.

6. Identify the photograph with an attached caption. Stamp your name and address on the back of all photos; don't write on the picture, especially with a ballpoint pen; you may ruin it. Photos containing a group should have the individuals identified from "left to right." Don't fold, crease, or write on the front of a photograph.

7. Package the news release and photo in a manila envelope and mail it to the attention of the New Products Editor. A letter is not necessary. You may send the same package to as many different magazines

as you feel would be interested in your product; but send them all at the same time. Editors don't take too kindly to receiving a news release later than their competitors.

If your product is newly developed or has been modified within the past 12 months, and if it has not previously been advertised, get going—you can probably get yourself a few hundred bucks worth of free magazine space.

free international publicity— uncle sam wants to help you

"You don't get something for nothing" is a truism we are all familiar with and in which we all believe. But if you have a product you would like to develop some international sales for, there really is something you can get for free—no strings attached, no hidden gimmicks—absolutely free.

The United States Department of Commerce offers a free export promotion service to help American companies. This service can be helpful to (1) publicize the availability of new U.S. products in foreign countries and (2) test overseas market interest in the particular new product.

The program is called New Product Information Service (NPIS). It's designed to encourage foreign companies to contact American companies about their new products. These contacts are helpful to American companies exploring foreign buyer interest and can result in actual product sales and the establishment of overseas agents. Products selected for this New Product Information Service are promoted in foreign markets through the following:

1. The Department of Commerce's "Commercial News USA" magazine (write for information). This magazine is sent regularly to 240 American Embassies and U.S. Consulates overseas. The new product information it contains (photos and write-ups) may be reprinted in as many as 70 Post Commercial Newsletters that have a combined distribution to over 100,000 foreign industry and government officials.

2. Voice of America radio broadcasts. The Voice of America radio simultaneously prepares global and regional broadcasts, called "New Products USA," in up to 37 languages.

Participation in the NPIS program can be beneficial to you. In a survey of 200 companies selected at random, it was determined the companies had received more than 6,500 foreign inquiries for their products as a result of having taken part in the NPIS program.

To participate in the program, companies must meet the following established "NPIS Criteria Guidelines."

I. Firms participating in NPIS must do the following:
   1. Want the product promoted worldwide (if a firm is not the manufacturer, it must have documented worldwide export rights to the product).
   2. Agree to answer promptly all overseas inquiries resulting from NPIS promotion.
   3. Not have promoted another product through NPIS during the past six months.
   4. Report on results of NPIS participation.

II. Products selected for NPIS will be restricted to those which:
   1. Are manufactured in the United States or 51% of its component value is of U.S. origin.
   2. Are labeled and marketed as U.S. products.
   3. Are genuinely new and with unique features, not marginal improvements of existing products.
   4. Have been offered for sale for less than two years on the U.S. market.
   5. Are presently exported to not more than three countries on a regular basis.
   6. Are immediately available for export orders worldwide.

If you are interested and think you qualify, contact the Department of Commerce, Domestic and International Business Administration, Bureau of International Commerce, Washington, D.C. 20230 (or your local district office) for detailed information and an NPIS application.

As I said before, it's free. And if you qualify, it's one of those rare opportunities for you, as a businessperson, to get something worthwhile from Uncle Sam.

TRUTH
IN ADVERTISING

how to stay out
of legal hot water

You can fool some of the people all of the time, and you can fool all of the people some of the time, but you can't fool all of the people all of the time.

ABRAHAM LINCOLN (1809–1865)

If Mr. Lincoln were working in advertising today, he would revise his saying to read, "Don't try to fool any of the people any of the time." It would be good advice, too, because today, more than ever before, consumer protection agencies are clamping down on advertisers who are trying to rip off the public.

In *Madison Avenue* magazine, Ted Thompson, president of Ted Thompson & Partners, put it this way, "Too many people, in and out of our business, feel like they're being had. . . . If you share this anxiety . . . there is probably only one thing to do about it: tell the truth; be honest."

The Federal Trade Commission, the Federal Communications Commission, the U.S. Postal Service, the Food and Drug Administration, the Securities and Exchange Commission, and the Public Health Service are only a few of the governmental agencies involved in protecting the public against deceptive advertising claims. At the state level, there is the Attorney General's Office; and at the city level, consumers can register complaints with the District Attorney's Office.

Businesses that follow the old rule of "caveat emptor" (let the buyer beware) are flirting with courts governed by the legal principle of "caveat venditor" (let the seller beware).

When an advertiser makes a claim in an advertisement, it is a public promise and becomes a published public record for which he can be held accountable.

You're inviting a visit from one of the numerous consumer protection groups if your advertising does not make sufficient disclosure, leaves out information, does not disclose any risk or hazard of a product, or is patently unfair or deceptive.

Advertising Age magazine quoted Albert Kramer, of the FTC Consumer Protection Bureau, as saying, "There are a whole variety of ways we're going to be trying to reach the public about the problem of deceptive advertising." In the same publication, FTC's Michael Pertschuk suggested to advertising people that they use "open and honest dealing, and [make] an effort to see the problem in terms of its impact on the other fellow [the consumer]."

In the past few years, substantial restrictive legislation and rulings against false and misleading advertising have been set in motion to protect the public.

The Printer's Ink Model Statute,* relating to false and deceptive advertising practices, has been adopted by 27 states and the District of Columbia. In addition, 17 other states have modified it and made it law. Here is an excerpt from this statute:

> *Any person, firm, corporation or association or agent or employee thereof, who, with intent to sell, purchase or in any wise dispose of, or to contract with reference to merchandise, real estate, service, employment, or anything offered by such person, firm, corporation or association, or agent of employee thereof, directly or indirectly, to the public for sale, purchase, distribution, or the hire of personal services, or with intent to increase the consumption of or to contract with reference to any merchandise, real estate, securities, service, or employment, or to induce the public in any manner to enter into any obligation relating thereto, or to acquire title thereto, or interest therein, or to make any loan, makes, publishes, disseminates, circulates or places before the public, or causes, directly or indirectly, to be made, published, disseminated, circulated, or placed before the public, in this state, in a newspaper, magazine, or other publication, or in the form of a book, notice, circular, pamphlet, letter, handbill, poster, bill, sign, placard, card, label, or over any radio or television station or other medium of wireless communication, or in any other way similar or dissimilar to the foregoing, an advertisement, announcement or statement of any sort regarding merchandise, securities, service, employment, or anything so offered for use, purchase or sale, or the interest, terms or conditions upon which such loan will be made to the public, which advertisement contains any assertion, representation or statement of fact which is untrue, deceptive, or misleading, shall be guilty. . . .*

who's liable?

Advertisers and advertising agencies who are aware of and participate in a deceptive practice are liable, because they are usually involved in the marketing plans, gathering data, layouts, concepts, and

---

* Copyright 1959 by Printer's Ink Publishing Corporation.

preparation and placement of the advertising message. The retailer who receives and uses deceptive advertising can also be held accountable because he or she has the option not to use the material. In certain situations, media can be held responsible, and many have taken protective steps by not accepting questionable types of advertising.

The advertiser is responsible for all meanings that an advertising message communicates. Its advertising agency is jointly responsible for the substance of the advertising message. The agency must not merely accept information the client supplies but must gather its own data to substantiate the advertising claims it makes.

The advertiser and the agency have a duty to the public to do the following:

1. Refrain from advertising a product that is unsafe or potentially hazardous.

2. Refrain from false claims that lead a customer to expect a better product than he or she will actually get.

3. Refrain from creating false impressions—by the use of the word "free," or testimonials, or reduced special prices that are phony—in order to motivate sales.

4. Refrain from unfairly hurting competition through comparative advertising that disparages a competitor's products.

5. Refrain from making claims for a product without substantiation or some reasonable basis for making such claims.

Fooling the customer these days is a risky and expensive proposition.

Nation's Business magazine reported, "Two trends have been major contributors to the product liability problem. (1) There has been a significant shift in product liability law; it now favors the plaintiffs over the defendant. (2) In recent years the consumerism movement has encouraged the public to sue and judges and juries to make large demand awards."

According to an article in *Industrial Marketing* magazine, "The average product liability judgment in many parts of the U.S. now is over $150,000." And the Insurance Information Institute reported that insurance companies have lost almost $9 billion on product liability claims in three years (1974 to 1976).

"A company's best protection against product liability will be the strict attention it pays to the quality and safety of its products and the adequacy of disclosure in the marketing and advertising programs," said

John J. Matternas, president of Insurance Management of Washington, Inc., in *Nation's Business* magazine.

the federal trade commission

The Federal Trade Commission (FTC) is an independent law enforcement agency charged by Congress with protecting the public—consumers and businesspeople alike—against anticompetitive behavior and unfair and deceptive business practices.

Headquartered in Washington, D.C. it has regional offices located in various parts of the country. In addition to their other responsibilities, the FTC defines practices that violate the law so business people may know their legal obligations and consumers may recognize those business practices against which legal recourse is available.

The FTC exercises its corrective responsibility by issuing complaints and entering orders to halt false advertising or fraudulent selling or to prevent a businessperson or corporation from using unfair tactics against competitors. The Commission itself has no authority to imprison or fine. However, if one of its final cease and desist orders or trade regulation rules is violated, it can seek civil penalties in federal court of up to $10,000 a day for each violation. It can also seek redress for those who have been harmed by unfair or deceptive acts or practices. Redress may include cancellation or reformation of contracts, refunds of money, return of property, and payment of damage.

It can also serve an order for corrective advertising in the form of retractions of false advertising claims for the next 25% of all of a violator's advertising, or it can have the violator publish corrective statements or ads in the same number as the false ads.

The Federal Trade Commission has booklets available that offer guides designed to "highlight certain problems in the field of advertising which experience has demonstrated to be especially troublesome to business people who in good faith desire to avoid deception of the consuming public." The guides are not intended to serve as comprehensive or precise statements of law, but rather as practical aids to the businessperson who seeks to conform his or her conduct to the requirements of fair and legitimate merchandising. They are *offered as guides only* and *not as fixed rules* of 'do's' and 'don'ts,' or *detailed statements* of the Commission's enforcement policies." Here are some excerpts.

guides against deceptive pricing

One of the most commonly used forms of bargain advertising is to offer a reduction from the advertiser's own former price for an article. If the former price is the actual, bona fide price at which the article was offered to the public on a regular basis for a reasonably substantial period of time, it provides a legitimate basis for the advertising of a price comparison. If, on the other hand, the former price being advertised is not bona fide but fictitious—for example, where an artificial, inflated price was established for the purpose of enabling the subsequent offer of a large reduction—the "bargain" being advertised is false; the purchaser is not receiving the unusual value expected.

The following is an example of a price comparison based on a fictitious former price. John Doe is a retailer of Brand X fountain pens, which cost him $5 each. His usual mark-up is 50% over cost; that is, his regular retail price is $7.50. In order subsequently to offer an unusual "bargain," Doe begins offering Brand X at $10 per pen. He realizes that he will be able to sell no, or very few, pens at this inflated price. But he doesn't care, for he maintains that price for only a few days. Then he "cuts" the price to its usual level—$7.50—and advertises: "Terrific Bargain: X Pens, Were $10, Now Only $7.50!" This is obviously a false claim. The advertised "bargain" is not genuine.

The practices covered in the provisions set forth above represent the most frequently employed forms of bargain advertising. However, there are many variations that appear from time to time and that are, in the main, controlled by the same general principles. For example, retailers should not advertise a retail price as a "wholesale" price. They should not represent that they are selling at "factory" prices when they are not selling at the prices paid by those purchasing directly from the manufacturer. They should not offer seconds or imperfect or irregular merchandise at a reduced price without disclosing that the higher comparative price refers to the price of the merchandise if perfect. They should not offer an advance sale under circumstances where they do not, in good faith, expect to increase the price at a later date, or make a "limited" offer that, in fact, is not limited. In all of these situations, as well as in others too numerous to mention, advertisers should make certain that the bargain offer is genuine and truthful. Doing so will serve their own interests as well as that of the public.

guides concerning
use of the word "free"
and similar representations

When making "free" or similar offers, all the terms, conditions, and obligations upon which receipt and retention of the "free" item are contingent should be set forth clearly and conspicuously at the outset of the offer so as to leave no reasonable probability that the terms of the offer might be misunderstood. For example, disclosure of the terms of the offer set forth in a footnote of an advertisement to which reference is made by an asterisk or other symbol placed next to the offer is not regarded as making disclosure at the outset. However, mere notice of the existence of a "free" offer on the main display panel of a label or package is not precluded provided that (1) the notice does not constitute an offer or identify the item being offered "free"; (2) the notice informs the customer of the location, elsewhere on the package or label, where the disclosures required by this Guide may be found; (3) no purchase or other such material affirmative act is required in order to discover the terms and conditions of the offer; and (4) the notice and the offer are not otherwise deceptive.

    Offers of "free" merchandise or services that may be deceptive for failure to meet the provisions of this Guide may not be corrected by the substitution of such similar words and terms as "gift," "given without charge," "bonus," or other words or terms that tend to convey the impression to the consuming public that an article of merchandise or service is "free."

guides against bait advertising

Bait advertising is an alluring but insincere offer to sell a product or service that the advertiser in truth does not intend or want to sell. Its purpose is to switch consumers from buying the advertised merchandise in order to sell something else—usually at a higher price or on a basis more advantageous to the advertiser. The primary aim of a bait advertisement is to obtain leads as to persons interested in buying merchandise of the type so advertised.

    Bait Advertisement: No advertisement containing an offer to sell a product should be published when the offer is not a bona fide effort to sell the advertised product.

172

Initial Offer: No statement or illustration should be used in any advertisement that creates a false impression of grade, quality, make, value, currency of model, size, color, usability, or origin of the product offered, or that may otherwise misrepresent the product in such a manner that later, on disclosure of the true facts, the purchaser may be switched from the advertised product to another.

Even though the true facts are subsequently made known to the buyer, the law is violated if the first contact or interview is secured by deception.

Sales of Advertised Merchandise: Sales of the advertised merchandise do not preclude the existence of a bait and switch scheme. It has been determined that, on occasions, this is a mere incidental byproduct of the fundamental plan and is intended to provide an aura of legitimacy to the overall operation.

Inquiries and requests for copies of these Guides should be directed to the Division of Rules and Guides, Federal Trade Commission, Washington, D.C. 20580.

common-sense rules that can help you tip-toe through the legal mine field

1. Be truthful at all times. Advertising must not only tell the truth, but the impression the consumer gets should be accurate. "If you are out to describe the truth, leave elegance to the tailor," said Albert Einstein. The courts hold that the overall impression an advertisement projects is the determining factor as to whether or not it is false or misleading. Inferences, half-truths, and doubletalk will not do. Statements must be so clear the average user with limited intelligence could not be confused by it. For example, if you were claiming, "These are the lowest-priced shoes offered," you should change it to, "The lowest-priced shoes we have ever offered."

Consider the ad or campaign, in terms of the total impression it conveys to the customer. Are the pictures honest? Is the type too small? Are the words clear and without a tendency to mislead? Is the message truthful but open to interpretation? Are the statements ambiguous, if not out and out false?

2. Document all claims. Claims regarding a product or service should have proof to back them up. There is increased demand for adver-

tisers to have documentation available on claims relating to "the safety, performance, and efficacy of their products."

And substantiation must be in existence at the time a claim is made—not afterwards. Even if you could prove a statement after the fact, it may not be accepted as evidence if you get into court.

3. Demonstrate products honestly. The product demonstrated must be exactly the same as the one the purchaser will get. Products used for advertising purposes should be taken from the production line. And photos of the product should not be retouched to conceal any defects. Toy demonstrations must be such that the average child, for whom the product is intended, can duplicate the demonstration—don't kid the kids.

4. Keep testimonials honest. Personal endorsements should be genuine and reflect personal experiences. Don't include a statement that cannot be supported if presented in the advertiser's own words.

5. Stand behind your guarantee. In general, any guarantee in advertising should clearly and conspicuously disclose (1) the nature and extent of the guarantee; (2) the manner in which the guarantor will perform; and (3) the identity of the guarantor.

6. Don't use the word "free" unless you really mean it. If there are any terms or conditions for getting something free, they must be obviously stated along with the word "free." Accordingly, whenever a "2-for-1," "half-price sale," "1¢ sale," 50% off," or similar type of offer is made, all the terms and conditions of the offer should be made clear at the outset.

7. Be sure you are aware of your company's advertising claims and approve of them. When in doubt, have your lawyer offer an opinion.

8. Keep up with consumer protection legislation that relates to your business. Regulations by federal, state, and city governments are constantly changing; be sure you have the latest information.

The legal ramifications of advertising need not concern you if you follow one of humanity's oldest laws, "Do unto others as you would have others do unto you."

If you would like more information on the subject, write to the Distribution and Duplication Branch, Federal Trade Commission, Washington, D.C. 20580, for a free copy of their "List of Publications."

MEDIA
INFORMATION:
WHERE TO FIND IT

standard rate & data service—
a treasury of media information

When up-to-date media information is needed to prepare an advertising budget, plan a schedule of advertisements, or purchase individual ad space, do what advertising agencies do; look up the information in a Rate & Data Service directory (see Figure 14–1).

Standard Rate & Data Service, Inc. (SRDS) publishes individual books that contain current, concise, and comprehensive media data that are extremely helpful to advertisers. These publications include information on advertising rates, circulation figures, mechanical requirements, issuance and closing dates, marketing data, circulation coverage, and other important data for use in estimating ad budgets and preparing schedules. Most of the directories are published monthly and updated with "Change Bulletins" that are issued weekly.

Listings in each directory are compiled under a uniform group of headings. In addition to a publisher's editorial profile that describes the medium, each listing contains the following data in this numerical sequence:

1. Personnel—editor, publisher, and executives with responsibility relative to advertising.
2. Representatives and/or Branch Offices—names, addresses, and phone numbers.
3. Commissions and Cash Discounts—amounts and availabilities of commissions and discounts.
4. General Rate Policy—rates, contract cancellation clause, policy on rate protection and rate revision.
5. Black-and-White Rates—rates including discount structures.
   5a. Combination Rates—availability of combination rates.
   5b. Discounts (Gross Expenditures)—discounts applicable to total dollars invested.
6. Color Rates—if available, rates for standard or selected colors, and structures for discounts.
7. Covers—rates, if available.
8. Inserts (Magazines)—rates and special charges.
9. Bleed—space and color charge, gutter bleed for magazines.
10. Special Position—availability, rates, and spreads.
11. Classified and Reading Notices—rates for classified ads, reading notices, display classifications, and mail order.
12. Split-Run—rates and requirements.

176

1—ADVERTISING & Marketing

Also see the following related Classifications

ADVERTISING AGE
(incorporating Promotion)
A Crain Communications, Inc. Publication

ABC MPA ★ABP

Media Code 7 005 0240 4.00
Published weekly by Crain Communications, Inc., 740 N. Rush St., Chicago, Ill. 60611. Phone 312-649-5200.
For shipping info., see Print Media Production Data.

1. PERSONNEL
Publisher—Lou DeMarco.
Advertising Director—David Persson.
Director Marketing Services—R. Bersin.
Production Manager—Elmer Kerstowske.

2. REPRESENTATIVES and/or BRANCH OFFICES
New York 10017—Joseph Doherty, Eastern Sales Manager, 708 Third Ave. Phone 212-986-5050.
Chicago 60611—Richard I. Kean, Midwest Sales Mgr., 740 Rush. Phone 312-649-5809.
Los Angeles 90048—James S. Mills, Western Sales Mgr., 6404 Wilshire Blvd. Phone 213-651-3710.

3. COMMISSION AND CASH DISCOUNT
15% of gross billing to recognized agencies on space, color, bleed and position, provided account is paid within 30 days of invoice date. Bills are dated Monday, same day as publication. Commission not allowed on mechanical charges and classified advertising. Cash Discount—2% on net (after agency commission) if paid 15 days after invoice date. U. S. funds. Discount allowed on current bills only.

4. GENERAL RATE POLICY
When new rates are announced, contract advertisers will be protected at their contract rates for 90 days after effective date of new rate. Orders beyond three months accepted at rates prevailing.

ADVERTISING RATES
Effective October 1, 1978. (Card No. 39.)
Card received September 29, 1978.

5. BLACK/WHITE RATES

	1 ti	6 ti	13 ti	26 ti
1 pg (70")	3279.50	3195.50	3111.50	3027.50
56 inches	2657.20	2590.00	2522.80	2455.60
48 inches	2306.40	2248.80	2191.20	2133.60
42 inches	2018.10	1967.70	1917.30	1866.90
40 inches	1922.00	1874.00	1826.00	1778.00
35 inches	1681.75	1639.75	1597.75	1555.75
30 inches	1441.50	1405.50	1369.50	1333.50
14 inches	681.10	664.30	647.50	630.70
†10 inches	486.50	474.50	462.50	450.50
7 inches	344.75	336.35	327.95	319.55
1 inch	48.05	46.85	46.85	45.65
*96 inches (Jr. spread)	4612.80	4497.60	4382.40	4267.20
*140 inches (2-page spread)	6559.00	6391.00	6223.00	6055.00
	39 ti	52 ti	65 ti	
1 pg (70")	2985.50	2943.50	2901.50	
56 inches	2422.00	2388.40	2354.80	
48 inches	2104.80	2076.00	2047.20	
42 inches	1841.70	1816.50	1791.30	
40 inches	1754.00	1730.00	1706.00	
35 inches	1534.75	1513.75	1492.75	
30 inches	1315.50	1297.50	1279.50	
14 inches	622.30	613.90	605.50	
†10 inches	444.50	438.50	432.50	
7 inches	315.35	311.15	306.95	
1 inch	45.05	44.45	43.85	
*96 inches (Jr. spread)	4209.60	4152.00	4094.40	
*140 inches (2-page spread)	5971.00	5887.00	5803.00	

Number of insertions used within 12 months from date of first insertion of contract period determines frequency rate.
(*) Full or fractional page spread ads are charged for at rate of each individual unit on each facing page. Multiple units of space in one issue are charged for at individual unit rates and are counted as individual units for the purpose of determining frequency discount.
(†) Rateholder.

INCH RATE (per inch)

	1 ti	6 ti	13 ti	26 ti
70 (1 pg)	46.85	45.65	44.45	43.25
50 to 70	47.45	46.25	45.05	43.85
30 to 50	48.05	46.85	46.85	44.45
10 to 30	48.65	47.45	46.25	45.05
1 to 10	49.25	48.05	46.85	45.65
	39 ti	52 ti	65 ti	
70 (1 pg)	42.65	42.05	41.45	
50 to 70	43.25	42.65	42.05	
30 to 50	43.85	43.25	42.65	
10 to 30	44.45	43.85	43.25	
1 to 10	45.05	44.45	43.85	

5a. COMBINATION RATES
Insertions in Advertising Age and Industrial Marketing may be combined within same contract year to obtain best earned frequency rate for each publication. Frequency discount is subject to minimum rateholder regulation applying in each for rate-holder units of space or larger.

6. COLOR RATES
Available with units of 14 column inches and larger.

Standard red, blue, green, yellow, extra per color, per page, over space cost	305.
Per spread, same color, extra	435.
Matched colors, not including metallic, extra	360.
Per spread, same color	520.
Metallic colors, per page, extra	290.
4-color process, per page	1080.
Per spread	1560.

7. COVERS
1st covers gatefolds (3 pages, 4 colors) in specified issues 18,875.00.
1st cover gatefolds (3 pages, black and white) in specified issues 17,000.00.
Section 2:
1st cover gatefold (3 pages, 4 colors) 17,000.00.
1st cover gatefolds (3 pages, black and white) 15,300.00.

8. INSERTS
1 and 2 page inserts that are standard full page size, or undersize larger in area than 1/2 page (81 square inches), full page rates apply. Undersize inserts should be supplied finish-trimmed to size desired.
Mechanical charges:

Single leaf (printed one side)	540.
Single leaf (printed 2 sides)	150.
Double leaf (with blank page or pages)	540.
Double leaf (no blank pages)	150.
All others—available.	
Inserts requiring special trimming, extra	300.

9. BLEED
Acceptable in spreads, full pages or multiple full column units.
Bleed charge on space only................10%
No extra charge for spreads that bleed into gutter only.

10. SPECIAL POSITION
Page 4 (space unit must be 3 cols. x 10" and 2 col. x 5" to 7-1/2" only), extra................20%
Page 5, extra................20%
Other acceptable specified positions, extra........20%
Positions guaranteed only after consulting publisher as to availability and apply only on ads of 10" or more. Position charge on black and white space cost only.

11. CLASSIFIED AND READING NOTICES
Classified:
Per line (minimum 20.00)................5.00
Minimum ad 4 lines. Must be prepaid.
Rates same as R.O.P. display.
Deadline Tuesday noon, 6 days preceding publication date.
Page is 6 cols. 1 col. 1-5/8"; 2 cols. 3-3/8"; 3 cols. 5-1/8"; 4 cols. 6-7/8"; 5 cols. 8-5/8"; 6 cols. 10-3/8".

13. SPECIAL ISSUE RATES AND DATA
AGENCY INCOME ISSUE
Published Spring.
100 LEADING NATIONAL ADVERTISERS ISSUE
Published Summer.
100 LEADING MARKETS ISSUE
Published Fall.
Rates and closing dates available.

13a. GEOGRAPHIC and/or DEMOGRAPHIC EDITIONS
Effective January 21, 1980. (Card No. 5a.)
Card received March 11, 1980.

Regional rates:	1 ti	6 ti	13 ti
Eastern	2093.00	2051.00	2009.00
Midwestern	1610.00	1582.00	1554.00
Southern	1067.50	1046.50	1025.50
Western	1067.50	1046.50	1025.50
	26 ti	39 ti	52 ti
Eastern	1967.00	1946.00	1925.00
Midwestern	1526.00	1512.00	1498.00
Southern	1004.50	994.00	983.50

14. CONTRACT AND COPY REGULATIONS
See Contents page for location—item 32.

15. MECH. REQUIREMENTS (Web Offset)
For complete, detailed production information, see SRDS Print Media Production Data.
Trim size: 11 x 14-3/4; No./Cols. 5.
Binding method: Saddle Stitched.
Colors available: AAAA/ABP; Matched; 4-Color Process (AAAA/MPA): Simulated Metallic.

DIMENSIONS—AD PAGE

1 pg. 10-1/4	x 14	3 col. 6	x 14
1 col. 1-7/8	x 14	4 col. 8-1/8	x 14
2 col. 4	x 14	5 col. 10-1/4	x 14

Spreads:

6 col.	6-3/8 x 14	Center spread	
8 col.	8-3/8 x 14	21	x 14
10 col.	10-1/2 x 14		

16. ISSUE AND CLOSING DATES
Published weekly; issued Monday.
Last forms close (in Chicago) Thursday, 11 days preceding date of publication. Last forms for Section 2 close (in Chicago) Monday, 14 days preceding date of issue. When proofs must be submitted for O.K. copy, or artwork, must be in hands of publisher 2 weeks preceding date of insertion.

17. SPECIAL SERVICES
MCC Media Data Form registered 6/21/78.

18. CIRCULATION
Established 1930. Single copy .75; per year 25.00.
Summary data for detail see Publisher's Statement.
A.B.C. 12-31-78 (6 mos. aver.—Blue BP Form)

Total	Non-Pd	Paid (Subs)	(Single) [Assoc]
72,103		72,103 70,697	1,406

Average Other Distribution (not included above): Total 1,074

TERRITORIAL DISTRIBUTION 11/78—74,696
N.Eng. Mid.Atl. E.N.Cen. W.N.Cen. S.Atl. E.S.Cen.
4,099 20,953 15,620 4,500 6,717 1,673
W.S.Cen. Mtn.St. Pac.St. Canada Foreign Other
3,324 1,927 7,303 1,681 4,646 2,360

BUSINESS ANALYSIS OF CIRCULATION
TL Total.
1 —Manufacturers:
(1-1)—Heads of bus.—chairmen & v-chairmen, pres., partners & owners.
(1-2)—Vice-presidents.
(1-3)—Secretaries & treasurers.
(1-4)—General managers.
(1-5)—Sales managers.
(1-6)—Adv. mgrs. (incl. sales promotion mgrs., dirs. of publicity, dirs. of public relations).
(1-7)—Territorial division & branch subs. (incl. 504 subs. with title of mgr., sales mgr., adv. mgr. or above).
(1-8)—Misc. execs. & all other home office employes.
(1-9)—Subscriptions in co. name.
2 —Wholesalers, distrs., jobbers incl. their pers.
3 —Public utilities (electric, gas, telephone, etc.), also local transp. cos. incl. their pers.
4 —Banks, financial underwriters & investment houses incl. their pers.
5 —Trade assocs. & promotional groups incl. chambers of commerce incl. their pers.
6 —Retail establishments (incl. chain stores & mail order houses), local service cos. incl. their pers.
7 —Advertising agencies incl. their pers.
8 —Graphic arts & adv. services incl. their pers.
9 —Media incl. their personnel & reps.
(9-1)—Newspapers.
(9-2)—Magazines, farm & bus publications.
(9-3)—Radio & television.
(9-4)—All other.
10 —Schools & colleges—professors, students.
11 —Miscellaneous.
12 —Awaiting class. by bus. & ind.

TL	1	(1-1)	(1-2)	(1-3)	(1-4)	(1-5)
72552	15732	807	1633	59	494	2207
(1-6)	(1-7)	(1-8)	(1-9)	2	3	4
4927	691	3522	1392	1682	506	889
5	6	7	8	9	(9-1)	(9-2)
1112	6346	17492	8004	11179	2350	5139
(9-3)	(9-4)	10	11	12		
2907	783	5834	1767	2009		

Submitted by J. B. Carlson.

Fig. 14–1 Typical media information listing in Standard Rate & Data.
Courtesy Standard Rate & Data Service, Inc.

13. Special Issue Rates and Data—information concerning special issues (exclusive of regular issues).
    13a. Geographic and/or Demographic Editions—rates and requirements.
14. Contract and Copy Regulations.
15. Mechanical Requirements—ad page dimensions, ad sizes available, colors, and other production information.
16. Issuance and Closing Dates—frequency of publication, deadlines for space reservations and material for advertising.
17. Special Services—available from the publication.
18. Circulation—circulation figures for the publication.

Individual SRDS directories are available as follows:

1. Newspaper Rates and Data (12 issues): Profiles of U.S. newspaper and newspaper groups, edited and organized to serve the information needs of newspaper advertising buyers.

2. Newspaper Circulation Analysis (annual): A comprehensive compilation of circulation information needed to plot and rank newspapers and newspaper markets; designed as a working companion to Newspaper Rates and Data.

3. Business Publication Rates and Data (12 issues): Contains business, trade, and technical publications in the U.S.; with "market served" classifications. Includes international business publications frequently used by U.S. advertisers.

4. Consumer Magazine and Farm Publication Rates and Data (12 issues): Features consumer and farm publications. Arranged alphabetically in classifications by "editorial content."

5. Weekly Newspaper and Shopping Guide Rates and Data (2 issues): Contains sections on metropolitan, urban/suburban area newspapers, non-metro weekly newspapers and shopping guides.

6. Print Media Production Data (quarterly): Features production data for business, consumer, and farm publications and daily newspapers.

7. Transit Advertising Rates and Data (quarterly): Presents information on transit operators, arranged in geographical/alphabetical order. Includes addresses of branch offices, transit lines, communities served, card requirements, advertising rates, restrictions, and circulation in nine uniform, numerical headings, transportation, and advertising in Canada.

8. Spot Television Rates and Data (12 issues): Covers each television and regional network group alphabetically by state, city, and call letters. Includes special features, commissions, participating programs, rates, and station representatives.

9. Spot Radio Rates and Data (12 issues): Profiles AM and FM stations by state, city, and call letters. Includes basic planning and buying information, addresses, telephone numbers, and station representatives for almost every U.S. broadcasting station.

10. Spot Radio Small Markets Edition (2 issues): Contains information on radio stations in markets with a less than 25,000 population. Each listing includes call letters, address, phone, personnel, sales rep, programming format, facilities, network or group affiliation, time classification, and spot rate schedule.

11. Network Rates and Data (6 issues): Features information on national radio and television networks in metropolitan areas and network affiliations in other markets, discounts, production facilities, services, and closing times.

12. Direct Mail List Rates and Data (2 issues): Contains mailing lists and list selections available for rent and includes business lists, consumer lists, farm lists, co-op mailings, and package inserts. Arranged by market classification with description of the list, list source, rental rates, quantity, commission, restrictions, test arrangements, and method of addressing.

Standard Rate & Data Service, Inc. directories are available in the business reference section of most public libraries or by subscription through Standard Rate & Data Services, Inc., 5201 Old Orchard Road, Skokie, Illinois 60076.

ayer directory of publications

Would you believe there is a directory that has been compiling and listing the advertising media of this country for over 100 years? Well, there is. It's the *Ayer Directory of Publications*, published every year without interruption since 1869. It is the oldest and most widely used directory of its kind.

The *Ayer Directory of Publications* contains in-depth data on thousands of newspapers, magazines, and trade publications. It lists key personnel, circulation and marketing statistics, advertising rates, and other pertinent information on all qualified newspapers and general and special interest magazines in the United States (plus the District of Columbia, Puerto Rico, and the Virgin Islands), Canada, Bahamas, Bermuda, and the Republic of Panama and the Philippines. Included in the directory are special updated maps showing publication cities and towns.

The directory covers the following:

1. *Newspapers and magazines*—classified by state, town, province, or territory, with essential data about each publication and the city or town where it is published.

2. *Daily newspapers*—with circulation figures, addresses, and population of the coverage areas.

3. *Daily periodicals*—publications devoted chiefly to special market segments are listed by location, with circulation figures and area population.

4. *Weekly, semi-weekly, and tri-weekly newspapers*—alphabetical listing by state and town, including circulation and population of coverage area.

5. *Feature editors*—names, addresses, and phone numbers of the feature editors of newspapers with 100,000-plus circulation.

6. *Magazines of general circulation*—grouped according to classification, with circulation figures and a brief description of the publication's editorial content.

7. *Agricultural publications*—listed by classification, by state, and with circulation.

8. *College publications*—arranged by location, with circulation figures.

9. *Foreign language publications*—listed according to language, with circulation figures and locations.

10. *Black publications*—put in order by location, with circulation figures.

11. *Jewish publications*—by classification, location, and with circulation figures.

12. *Trade, technical, and professional publications*—grouped by special-interest fields, with circulation and location.

13. *Fraternal publications*—fraternal order, location, and circulation.

The *Ayer Directory* uses ten classes of circulation audits and statements to ensure the accuracy of the information contained in the book. Each circulation figure is the most recent and accurate figure available at press time. The latest address for each publication, complete with zip code, is printed. Additional information includes market and economic profiles of publication cities and towns and facts on population, agriculture, and industry. The directory contains accurate, up-to-date facts throughout its pages.

The *Ayer Directory* has earned a reputation as the unique, basic reference tool for print media by its thousands of professional users in research, public relations, advertising, trade associations, journalism, education, publishing, and so on. John C. Mansfield, Lloyd Mansfield Company, Inc., calls it "the most complete directory for information of this type."

If you would like more information, you may write to *Ayer Directory of Publications*, Ayer Press, 210 West Washington Square, Philadelphia, Pennsylvania 19106.

15

WHERE TO FIND
MORE INFORMATION

The most valuable result of all education is the ability to make yourself do
the thing you have to do, when it ought to be done.

THOMAS HENRY HUXLEY (1825–1895)

It probably first happened in 2001 B.C., at Happy Hairy's Used Dinosaur
lot, when the owner, Amos Hairy, who really was never very happy,
walked up to one of his unsuspecting employees and announced, "I'm
putting you in charge of our advertising." Since that time, the word
"advertising" has baffled countless newcomers who have been dumped,
unceremoniously, into the cold world of advertising without any preparation. All they can think of is "I don't know anything about advertising."

    If you're new to advertising, or even if you've been "doing it
for years," you may need help sometimes. This book should get you over a
lot of the bumps, but there are a number of other places for you to find
additional information.

    First, there's the public library. In the business section of
most libraries, you can find a good collection of self-help advertising books.
These are books written by professionals on almost every aspect of advertising. There are books on selling by direct mail, retail advertising, sales
promotions, window display, point of purchase, marketing, and so on. If
you need help in the artistic end of advertising, try the "graphics" section,
a separate department where you'll find the commercial art books. There
you'll discover books containing reproductions of the best ads from previous years; books on how to lay out your advertisement; and guides to
photography, typesetting, and the various printing processes. In the library's business reference section, you can find *Standard Rate & Data*, a
very handy monthly publication that contains much of the media information necessary for an ad person to prepare an advertising budget. Excellent, informative, helpful books are in the library for you to use. Use them.

    If you prefer to have a book at your fingertips at all times, try
a large bookstore in your city. I'm not sure why, but most bookstores don't
carry much in the way of books on advertising; they will be glad to special
order what you want, however. I suggest you start with either *Advertising
Procedure*, by Otto Kleppner, or *Advertising*, by Maurice I. Mandell. Both
are hardcover books and are published by Prentice-Hall. They cover the
field of advertising subject by subject, chapter by chapter. If you're trying
to understand the art and production side of the business, try *Advertising
Graphics*, by William Bockus, Jr., from Macmillan Publishing Co., or *The
Design of Advertising*, by Roy Paul Nelson, published by Wm. C. Brown
Company, Publishers. All of the above books are heavily illustrated and
are not difficult to read.

Advertising trade magazines are another good source of interesting information for both the newcomer or the ad professional. They contain news, feature articles, and a great deal of "how-to" material, on a current basis. Some of the more popular publications you can subscribe to are:

1. *Advertising Age*, 740 No. Rush St., Chicago, Illinois 60611, a national weekly magazine all the pros read to keep up to date on marketing, selling, ad campaigns, communications, merchandising, product positioning, research, and the like.

2. *Adweek Magazine*, 230 Park Ave., New York, New York 10017, available in regional editions, is edited for the area it serves and reports on local and national advertising news; it also includes many worthwhile articles on advertising.

3. *Art Direction Magazine*, 10 East 39th St., New York, New York 10016, geared to the interests of the visual advertiser, contains material on new techniques, services, and products in the graphics field.

4. *Broadcasting Magazine*, 1735 De Sales St., N.W., Washington, D.C. 20036, comes out weekly and covers radio and television business news on both a national and regional basis.

5. *Graphics Today*, 6 East 43rd St., New York, New York 10017, is a bi-monthly publication featuring profiles on professional people and their approach to solving graphic problems.

6. *Industrial Marketing*, 633 Third Ave., New York, New York 10017, concentrates on the new techniques and methods of advertising and selling products or services to business and industry.

7. *Marketing Communications*, 475 Park Ave. So., New York, New York 10016, covers advertising media, public relations, promotions, direct mail, premiums, and presentations.

8. *Television/Radio Age*, 1270 Avenue of the Americas, New York, New York 10020, is edited for both buyers and sellers of television and radio time.

These are just a handful of the trade publications whose content is advertising related. Write to any of these magazines for their subscription rates and a free sample copy. Read through them; if they can be helpful, sign up.

If reading is not your bag, look into classes offered by your local adult education, college, or university extension programs. If you can't find any courses on advertising as such, try market research, commercial art, creative writing, business administration, journalism, photography, selling, and even psychology; they will come in handy. Adams said, "I find that a great part of the information I have acquired was by looking up something and finding something else on the way."

Workshops and seminars offered by private organizations can provide an instant infusion of advertising information for the person who needs help in a hurry. Different programs are conducted in major cities throughout the country all year long. They offer a means of meeting other ad people with similar problems and an opportunity to ask questions of a working professional. The fee usually covers course materials, refreshments, and luncheon. To be put on a mailing list and notified of upcoming seminars in your area, write to: GATF, 4615 Forbes Ave., Pittsburgh, Pennsylvania 15213; Dynamic Graphics, 6707 No. Sheridan Road, Peoria, Illinois 61614; American Management Associations, 135 W. 50th St., New York, New York 10020; Crain Educational Division, 740 Rush St., Chicago, Illinois 60611; and Performance Seminars Group, 61 So. Division St., New Rochelle, New York 10801.

Whether it's through books, magazines, classes, or seminars, advertising should be a continual, enlightening experience for you. In the fast-paced world of advertising, learning is an ongoing process for all of us. M. M. Coady summed it up well, "The person who has ceased to learn ought not be allowed to wander around loose." Never cease to learn.

where to write for information

If you have need for further information on any advertising subject, I suggest you write to one or more of the appropriate organizations listed below for a list of available publications. Some of the publications they offer are free, whereas others may require a nominal fee.

Address your request to the "Publications Department." If you can, specify the type of information you are seeking.

The Advertising Checking Bureau, Inc.
434 South Wabash Avenue
Chicago, Illinois 60615

The Advertising Council
825 Third Avenue
New York, New York 10022

Advertising Research Foundation (ARF)
3 East 54 Street
New York, New York 10022

Agricultural Publisher's Association (APA)
111 East Wacker Drive
Chicago, Illinois 60601

American Advertising Federation
1225 Connecticut Avenue, N.W.
Washington, D.C. 20036

American Association of Advertising Agencies
200 Park Avenue
New York, New York 10017

American Business Press, Inc.
205 East 42 Street
New York, New York 10017

American Marketing Association (AMA)
222 South Riverside Plaza
Chicago, Illinois 60606

American Research Bureau (Arbitron)
4320 Ammendale Road
Beltsville, Maryland 20705

Association of National Advertisers
155 East 44 Street
New York, New York 10017

Association of Publishers' Representatives (APR)
850 Third Avenue
New York, New York 10022

Audit Bureau of Circulations (ABC)
123 North Wacker Drive
Chicago, Illinois, 60606

Ayer Directory of Publications
210 West Washington Square
Philadelphia, Pennsylvania 19106

Business Publications Audit of Circulation, Inc. (BPA)
360 Park Avenue South
New York, New York 10010

Certified Audit of Circulations, Inc. (CAC)
353 Broad Avenue
Leonia, New Jersey 07605

Council of Better Business Bureaus
1150 Seventeenth Street, N.W.
Washington, D.C. 20036

Direct Mail—Marketing Association
6 East 43 Street
New York, New York 10017

Gallup & Robinson, Inc. (Research)
Research Park
Princeton, New Jersey 08540

Home Testing Institute
50 Maple Place
Manhassett, New York 11030

Institute of Outdoor Advertising
485 Lexington Avenue
New York, New York 10017

International Advertising Association (IAA)
475 Fifth Avenue
New York, New York 10017

Magazine Publishers Association (MPA)
575 Lexington Avenue
New York, New York 10022

National Retail Merchants Association
100 West 31 Street
New York, New York 10001

Newspaper Advertising Bureau
485 Lexington Avenue
New York, New York 10017

A.C. Nielsen Company (Research)
Nielsen Plaza
Northbrook, Illinois 60062

Point of Purchase Advertising Institute
60 East 42 Street
New York, New York 10017

Alfred Politz Media Studies
300 Park Avenue South
New York, New York 10010

Radio Advertising Bureau
485 Lexington Avenue
New York, New York 10017

Sales and Marketing Executives Intl., Inc.
380 Lexington Avenue
New York, New York 10017

Sales Promotion Institute
200 Central Park South
New York, New York 10019

Selected Market Audit Division of BPA (SMA)
360 Park Avenue South
New York, New York 10010

Standard Rate & Data Service, Inc.
5201 Old Orchard Road
Skokie, Illinois 60076

Daniel Starch and Staff (Research)
420 Lexington Avenue
New York, New York 10017

Television Bureau of Advertising, Inc.
1345 Avenue of the Americas
New York, New York 10019

Traffic Audit Bureau, Inc.
708 Third Avenue
New York, New York 10017

Trendex, Inc. (Research)
800 Third Avenue
New York, New York 10022

Verified Audit Circulation Corporation (VAC)
1413 Seventh Street
Santa Monica, California 90401

u.s. government agencies

Department of Commerce
Washington, D.C. 20230

Federal Communication Commission (FCC)
1919 M Street, N.W.
Washington, D.C. 20554

Federal Trade Commission (FTC)
6th and Pennsylvania Avenue, N.W.
Washington, D.C. 20580

Food and Drug Administration (FDA)
Department of Health, Education, and Welfare
5600 Fishers Lane
Rockville, Maryland 20852

General Services Administration (GSA)
Consumer Information Center
1111 20th Street, N.W.
Washington, D.C. 20469

Occupational Safety and Health Administration (OSHA)
New Department of Labor
200 Constitution Avenue, N.W.
Washington, D.C. 20210

Office of Consumer Affairs
Executive Office Building
17th and Pennsylvania Ave., N.W.
Washington, D.C. 20201

Securities and Exchange Commission (SEC)
500 North Capitol Street
Washington, D.C. 20549

U.S. Small Business Administration
Washington, D.C. 20402

U.S. Consumer Product Safety Commission (CPSC)
Washington, D.C. 20207

U.S. Postal Service
Washington, D.C. 20260

QUESTIONS
AND ANSWERS

some frequently asked questions with answers

Q. Please help! I was running an ad in a local publication and decided to cancel it a couple of weeks ago. I called my sales representative and told him to discontinue it, but the ad is still appearing. Am I obligated to pay for the advertising I didn't want to run?

A. Relax. You are only responsible for what you authorize. Although it would have been better if you had sent written notice to cancel the ad, verbal instructions are valid. I suggest you follow up with a letter to the advertising manager explaining your conversation with the salesman; include the date you called and send the letter by certified mail. Like any good business, most publications want to satisfy their customers and will do what's fair.

Q. A friend and I recently discussed the rate of return we could expect on the money we spend for advertising. I said there's no set percentage we could count on as a return on our costs. My friend disagrees with me completely. Who's right?

A. You are. It would be nice to know that an advertiser might expect a predetermined amount as a return from his advertising; but, unfortunately, it's almost impossible. There are just too many variables that can affect the success or failure of an advertising program. For example, budget (are you spending enough to do the job?); ads (are your ads persuasive; too large; too small?); media (are the ads appearing in the right publications, the ones reaching good prospects for you, or is the money being wasted?); timing (is your advertising appearing when the customer is ready to buy, or are you trying to sell snowshovels in the summertime?). Like any investment, the rate of profit you can expect as a return depends on how well you invest your money.

Q. I recently graduated from school, and I'd like to find a job in advertising. I don't know exactly what I want to do, but I do know I don't want to be a secretary. Most of the openings I have come across seem to be for clerical help. How do you suggest I get started?

A. If you are talking about the larger agencies, chances are you would be pigeon-holed into a secretarial slot or some such clerical position. I would advise your looking into small advertising agencies, the one- or two-people shops who handle local advertising. A small agency owner cannot afford to have a person on the staff who does not wear many hats. Although the job might be classified as clerical, you probably would not only type, edit, and proofread copy; but you would most likely be asked to research media costs; send and follow up on ad insertions; requisition artwork, typography, and printing; and so on. In other words, you would be involved in every aspect of the agency business and you would learn what makes it tick. Jules B. Singer, in his book, *Your Future in Advertising*, said, "Your potential boss undoubtedly will want someone who takes initiative, who has leadership qualities, who gets along well with other people, who is loyal, who will do more than the routine job." If you have these traits, try the small agencies.

Q. My problem is time. Running my business, a retail store, takes up all of my days, but I'd still like to find out how to promote it. Is there any "quick" way to learn something about advertising?

A. There are several options for the businessperson on the go: (1) One-day advertising workshops or seminars are offered by some local colleges, newspapers, and the U.S. Small Business Administration. They are crammed with useful information designed for the small business. Some are free, depending on who is the sponsor, and they are usually given each year. (2) Adult education classes through community colleges and high schools are sometimes available on a one-evening-a-week basis, if you can spare the time. (3) Books, on every aspect of advertising, can be found in the business section of the public library. In addition, you should buy one book, at least, for easy reference. I recommend *Advertising*, Second edition, by Maurice I. Mandell; or *Advertising Procedure*, Sixth edition, by Otto Kleppner. Both are published by Prentice-Hall, Inc., Englewood Cliffs, New Jersey 07632.

Q. Is there anywhere I can find out how much advertising costs in different magazines without bothering with an advertising agency?

A. No problem. You can find all the information you probably need, and more, in copies of *Standard Rate & Data*, which supplies this type of information in a number of directories including ones on consumer magazines, business publications, newspapers, and so on. Another good source is the *Ayer Directory of Publications*. You can find one or both of these in the business reference section of the public library (see Chapter 14 for more information on these).

Q. Can you tell me who is liable for what we say in our advertising? I've heard it's the responsibility of our advertising agency, but I've always thought it's up to me, the advertiser. Which is right?

A. Both concepts are right. Under the law, an advertiser and its advertising agency are equally responsible for the claims made in an advertisement. As the client, you are responsible for providing factual information on your product(s) or service(s). Based on the information you supply, your ad agency is responsible for an accurate and truthful representation of the claims made in your advertising. In these days of growing consumer protection regulations, you cannot make dubious or exaggerated claims without having factual documentation to prove them. In addition, you cannot create any false or misleading impressions. Write to the Division of Legal and Public Records, Federal Trade Commission, Washington, D.C. 20580 for guidelines and a list of their publications on the subject.

Q. I'm interested in starting my own mail-order business; I have catalogs loaded with things I can sell by mail. How can I get started?
A. Go slowly; in fact, go very slowly. The business opportunities promoters claim that you can make large "profits in your spare time," but don't believe them. Mail order is one of the toughest businesses in which to make any money. You have to know about business licenses, property tax on inventories, estimating federal income taxes, ficticious name registration, IRS and State Department of Human Resources Development employer account numbers (if you hire someone), postal regulations, federal trade commission guidelines, and state laws limiting mail-order operations. Also, many magazines have their own regulations you must adhere to before they will accept your advertising. In addition, you have to constantly test and monitor your advertising program. Claude Hopkins, in his book, *Scientific Advertising*, said, "Mail order advertising is traced down to the fraction of a penny. It takes a lot of time, capital and discipline. The mail order business is no way to get rich quick." I strongly urge you to try some other business venture, about which you may know more.

Q. I own a small retail store and only have a limited amount of money I can afford to spend on advertising. Can you tell me when I should run my ads?
A. With weekly newspapers, it's best to advertise each week—or at least every other week—in order to develop some continuity in your advertising. In a daily paper, you have more options; I suggest you try the end of the week: Wednesdays, Thursdays, and Fridays, when people are planning to shop for the weekend. Try Friday first and work your way back toward the beginning of the week to find out which day is best for you. I suggest you avoid "Food Day" unless you're suited for this section. Just before a holiday weekend is a particularly good time for many retailers.

Q. My business has grown to a point where I just don't have the time to do everything myself anymore. Can you tell me what will be expected of me if I hire an advertising agency? Will they take the ball and run with it, or do I have to get involved?
A. If your business has been successful and has grown, it is probably due

in large measure to your leadership. The ability to lead is probably the single most important quality you will need to establish a good client/agency relationship. The agency will take the ball and run with it, as you suggest, but you should be prepared to do the following:

1. Give the agency some guidelines; tell them what you have been doing and what results you will be expecting from them. Be as specific as you can. If you want a 15% increase in sales, say so.

2. Get the agency involved in your business right away. Have a weekly (or monthly) meeting in your store. If you have more than one store, change location each time so the agency can meet more of your people and become familiar with your total operation.

3. Invite the copywriter to spend some time at one of your stores the day of a big sale. Have him or her sell merchandise, answer the phones, and so on in order to see, first hand, the results of his efforts.

4. Be complimentary when results warrant, but let the agency know when they are less than you expected. Don't be a nitpicker; tell them when you feel something is wrong, but don't try to tell them how to do it. Make the agency responsible for what they do.

5. Keep the approval system simple. Avoid decisions made by committee: It can demoralize an agency and waste a lot of time and money—yours.

Q. Several months ago I had a mailer printed that I used to send to potential customers. The mailers are all gone, and I need a new supply. I went back to the original printer, and he quoted me such a high price for reprinting that I decided to have someone else do it. My problem is that the original printer has my artwork. How do I get it back? Do I have to pay for it?

A. The artwork you supplied to the printer is your property and should have been returned to you with the original printed order. There is no reason why you simply can't ask for the return of your artwork without incurring any costs. In the event the printer lost or can't find your artwork, ask him to pay for having it redone, or, as an alternative, to supply you with the printing negatives. If you are not printing any major changes, the negatives will serve the same purpose as the artwork. Next time be sure to have your material returned with the printed order.

Q. I don't have an advertising department, and I can't afford to hire an agency or even an artist. So I have to do my own layouts, although I am not talented in this area. Can you give me some advice on how to make my ads look better and hopefully pull more?

A. Yours is a difficult question to answer in a few words. I have spent a great deal of time discussing the development of an effective layout (see Chapter 4). In addition, you can get some good layout ideas from "How To Make A Good Ad Better," a booklet put out by the Newspaper Advertising Bureau, Inc., 485 Lexington Avenue, New York, New York 10017. The cost is nominal, and it offers solutions to a variety of common layout problems. In advertising layouts it is especially important to remember the prime rule of advertising, "keep it simple."

Q. A radio salesman recently told me that his station was good compared to other media. I was embarrassed to ask what he meant by "media." Can you please tell me what the word means?

A. According to the *Ayer Glossary of Advertising and Related Terms*, media is defined as "vehicles for the dissemination of advertising and/or publicity and, more generally, news and information; principally includes publications, TV and radio, outdoor billboards and signs, transit cards and posters, movie trailers, direct mail, programs, etc."

Q. Help! I have just been told by my boss that I will be responsible for getting our monthly mailers printed. I can put them together easily, but I don't know anything about printing. Where can I get information?

A. Send for the *Pocket Pal*, an easy-to-read graphic arts production handbook. The 191-page book covers type and typesetting, copy and art preparation, inks, paper, and the entire printing process. *Pocket Pal* is available from the International Paper Company, 220 East 42nd Street, New York, New York 10017, for a small fee.

Q. Because of the variety of merchandise we sell, my partner and I have a difficult time deciding which items to advertise. Is there any "rule of thumb" guide for determining what is best to advertise?

A. Deciding on the proper item(s) to advertise is one of the most important decisions you can make to assure a successful promotion. To help determine what to promote, you should consider the following:

1. Merchandise that is popular with your customers and has proven to be a good seller in the past.
2. New merchandise on the market that is timely and for which your customers will be looking.
3. Seasonal items—swimwear for the summer, warm clothing for the winter, and so on.
4. Special merchandise priced to make it a good value anytime.

5. Brand items that have been heavily promoted by the manufacturer through national advertising.

Q. I have a nice drawing that I would like to use in my advertising, but it's too large to fit the size ad I can afford. Is there any way I can use it?

Q. You aren't restricted to using the drawing in the size it was made. You can have any artwork enlarged or reduced to whatever size you need at very little expense—usually only a few dollars. In your case, the easiest thing to do is give the drawing to the publication you are advertising in and tell them to reduce it to the size you want. They will photographically copy it and at the same time reduce it to the desired size. The print they make is called a stat, photoprint, or velox, depending on the detail in the drawing. Should you need duplicate copies of the entire ad to use in other publications, they can be made by the same method. Don't forget to have your original artwork returned, and keep it on file for future use.

Q. I'm thinking about offering a "special" and putting flyers on cars on large parking lots. What do you think about flyers: Are they worth the time and trouble?

A. No! I think putting flyers on the windshields of people's cars is a cheap way to irritate potential customers. Many people throw flyers away without even looking at them, thus creating a litter problem. For this reason, many cities have adopted ordinances against windshields flyers and consider their use a misdemeanor. If you are offering a genuine "special," you should be thinking about newspaper advertising.

Q. I have a small budget and have to get the most I can for my advertising money. Can you tell me, is it best to run one large ad in a newspaper, or should I run smaller ones and therefore appear more frequently?

A. That's a toughie to answer; so many factors have to be considered. Generally speaking, I think you can effectively use smaller ads, running them as frequently as your budget will allow. Because of their smaller size, your ads will have to work hard. Establish an ad format, such as a fancy border treatment or a distinctive art style, so that there is a continuing recognizable theme. Make one element, headline, photo, artwork, or logo very dominant so it jumps out of the page. But be flexible with your budget. When the occasion is right, such as Christmas time or holidays, don't hesitate to spend the money and go to a larger size ad. Since it is the time when people are spending money, you will want to increase your share of the available business.

GLOSSARY

ad terms and all that jazz

When it comes to communicating with the public, advertising people are the best in the world. They work hard to ensure that their messages are clear and concise. But when it comes to communicating with their own clients—the people who pay for the three-hour lunches and the lifetime supply of Alka Seltzer—advertising people rate a goose egg for contributing to the delinquency of the English language.

We, in advertising, unconsciously hit clients with jazzy jargon, fancy slang, and advertising buzz words. Instead of clarifying client communications, we merely add fuel to the confusion fire.

"You need to have a cut made of your head that bleeds" is a sample of the trade slang used by ad people. Translated, it means, "You need to have an engraving (cut) made of the headline (head) that extends to the edge of the paper (bleed)." An "engraving" or "cut" is also referred to as a "zinc," "plate," or "halftone"—just to confuse the issue further.

It's no small wonder that advertising terminology can sometimes be confusing and bewildering to the beginner. If you have difficulty understanding ad people who throw these zingers at you, the following list of some of the most common trade terms might be a help.

AAAA   American Association of Advertising Agencies. Also referred to as the "Four A's."

ABC   Audit Bureau of Circulation. An organization that verifies a publication's circulation figures.

ABP   Associated Business Publications. A trade-paper association.

AFTRA   American Federation of Television and Radio Actors and Actresses.

ANPA   American Newspaper Publisher's Association.

ARB   American Research Bureau. A television rating service.

accumulated audience (cumes)   The total number of people reached by a medium (print or broadcast) over a specified time period.

advertising   Any paid form of promotion of goods, services, or ideas by a known sponsor (advertiser).

agate line   A unit measurement by which the depth of advertising space is indicated and sold. There are 14 agate lines to the inch, one column wide. The column width will vary from publication to publication. Commonly referred to as a "line."

198

agency commission   A special discount allowed by media to recognized agencies for the advertising they place. Traditionally, it's 15% of space or time costs.

air brushing   A special technique to minimize or eliminate unwanted areas or blemishes in a photograph.

animation   A sequence of individual drawings (models, cartoons, puppets) photographed one frame at a time. When the film is run at a normal speed, it creates the illusion of movement.

art   Drawings, illustrations, cartoons, hand-lettering, or photographs that will be reproduced in an ad or printed piece.

artist   A specialist talented in rendering a form of art.

ascender   In lower-case letters, the stroke above the main portion of the letter, such as in "b," "d," and "h."

audio   The sound (only) portion of a television commercial or program.

author's alterations (A.A.)   Changes made by a client in material prior to reproduction; and not due to a typesetter's or printer's error. These are charged to client at a higher rate than the original work.

Ayer Directory of Publications   A reference source, listing newspapers and magazines.

BPA   Business Publications Audit. An organization that certifies circulation figures of business and trade publications.

B&W   abbreviation for "black-and-white."

bait advertising   A phony offer to sell a product with the intent of switching the customer to a more expensive product. Don't do it: The FTC is constantly after "bait and switch" advertisers.

Ben Day   A technique for creating a tonal effect by applying a dot or line pattern to a line drawing.

billboard   Popular name for a large outdoor advertising poster.

billings   The total cost for advertising space, time, and production incurred by an agency for a client. It is then rebilled to the client.

bleed   The printed part of an advertisement that runs to the very edge of the paper, leaving no margin. Artwork for "bleeds" usually extends for an extra ⅛ inch to allow for minor inaccuracies of printing, folding, binding, or trimming.

blow-up Englargement of a photograph, illustration, or type.

body type The main portion of the text set in type and used in an advertisement.

bold face (bf) A type style that is heavier in appearance than the regular type in its style.

broadside A large sheet of paper (usually 15 × 24 inches) printed on one side and folded to a smaller size for distribution.

brochure A bound pamphlet or booklet with multiple pages, used for sales promotion purposes.

brownline (also called a blueline) A checking proof made from the printer's offset film negatives before the final plate is made.

bulk mail Third class mail sent in quantity. Must be delivered to the post office in bundles and sorted by zip code. Check with your postmaster for complete regulations.

CPM (cost per thousand) Formula to determine how much it would cost to reach 1,000 people (readers, viewers, listeners) through a given medium. To calculate, divide (audience) into the media cost (rate).

CRA (camera-ready artwork) See "Key Line."

CU (close-up) Used in television commercials to indicate a compact camera shot to feature detail in a scene.

campaign A series of advertisements and related efforts designed to appear at regular intervals and with the same central selling idea or theme.

caps Capital letters in an alphabet. Also called "upper case."

caption Descriptive copy below a photograph or illustration. Also referred to as a "cut line."

characters Individual letters, numerals, and punctuation marks that make up the complete font (alphabet) of a type style.

checking copy A complete publication sent to an advertiser to confirm the appearance of an ad.

chroma-key A special electronic process by which the background scene in a TV commercial can be altered without affecting the foreground action.

circular Printed advertising material used for sales promotion activities.

circulation   The number of copies a periodical distributes of a single issue.

closing date (also called "deadline")   The last possible time an ad must be received by the media to guarantee its appearance in a specific issue.

color separations (also called "seps")   The four negatives (red, yellow, blue, and black) made from color art or photographs; needed for printing in full color.

color transparency   Color photograph on film, rather than paper. Also called a "Slide."

column inch   Unit of measure denoting an area of ad space one column wide by one inch deep.

combination rate   Special rate offered by publishers to advertisers placing the same ad in two or more publications, usually during a specified time period.

copy   The written or spoken words of the advertiser's message.

copywriter   The person who writes the words (copy) for an advertising message.

crop marks   Lines used to indicate those portions of artwork, photographs, or engravings to be eliminated. Crop marks are put in the margins around the materials—never directly on the material itself.

cut   A metal engraving used for letterpress printing. Also called a "zinc," "plate," or "halftone."

DMMA   Direct Mail-Marketing Association.

deadline   See "Closing Date."

descender   In lower-case letters, the stroke below the main portion of the letter, such as in "p," "q," and "y."

die cut   Various shapes and holes cut out of a printed page by the printer.

direct mail   Advertising or sales promotion material mailed directly to a potential customer.

display advertising   Newspaper advertising other than classified advertising.

display type   Type larger than 14 points (72 points = 1 inch) in size. Used in headlines, for example.

double truck   A single advertisement that covers two facing pages in a publication.

duotone   Photograph printed in two different colors.

ECU   Abbreviation for "extreme close-up." Used in television commercials to indicate a camera shot that shows the detail of a single section of an object or person.

edit   To prepare, clean up, and set in order copy for publication or reproduction.

editorial   News material in a publication, as distinguished from the advertising.

elite   A typewriter type size that has 12 letters (characters) to the inch.

em   A unit of measure in typesetting indicating the square of a type character, usually the "M".

en   A unit of measure, half of an em (see above).

English   Language to be used against ad-slang slingers. It's vital for you to know what's going on; don't be afraid to use the phrase, "What do you mean?"

engraving   Also referred to as a "zinc," or "cut," or "plate."

estimate   A preliminary projection of cost that is not intended to be binding. Also referred to as a "Guesstimate."

FCC   Federal Communications Commission.

FDA   Food and Drug Administration.

FM (frequency modulation)   A static-free, non-fading "band" for broadcasting.

FTC   Federal Trade Commission.

fee   A charge, not covered by the 15% commission, made by an advertising agency to a client for its services.

final proof   Copy of the completed advertisement as it will appear in the publication or printed piece.

finished art   The completed artwork for an advertisement, ready to be reproduced.

flat rate   A rate for space in a medium that doesn't have a discount.

flyer   A single sheet of paper printed on one side with an advertising message.

four-color process   Reproduction of color illustrations or photos with a set of four plates: yellow, red, blue, and black. These basic colors are combined to create the complete color range.

free-lance   Self-employed artists, writers, photographers, and the like who contract for their services by the project and are not employed by the hiring company.

GRP (gross rating points)   The number of rating points a program achieves on each station multipled by the times it runs within a given time period. Used to measure the audience of a station. Go slowly when you try to figure it out; the pros have trouble understanding it too.

galley proofs   Typeset copy of the manuscript, before it is assembled into page position (page proofs).

glossy (photo)   Photograph with a shiny surface. Preferred for most reproduction purposes.

gripper   The margin area (¼ inch or less) on a sheet of paper that is gripped by the press during the printing process.

gutter   The blank space (margins) between facing pages in a publication.

halftone   An illustration or photograph that has continuous (varying) tones of gray. When made into an engraving, it's called a "halftone plate."

headline   Short statement, larger in size than the body copy, in a conspicuous position within an ad. Usually found at the top of the ad.

house agency   An advertising agency owned in part, or completely, by an advertiser.

ID (identification spot)   Refers to either (1) a ten-second commercial or (2) a broadcast station identification announcement between programs.

imprint   The printed name or symbol of an advertiser on sales promotion material to identify the firm producing or distributing it.

indicia   The advertiser's postal permit number printed on an envelope or mailing piece in place of a stamp.

insertion order   Written authorization from an advertiser or ad agency to the media to carry advertising as specified at a published or agreed-upon rate.

island position   The placement of an ad (usually ½-page in size) within a periodical so that it is entirely surrounded by editorial matter.

italic   Letter(s) that are slanted.

justified   Type that is set to a specified measure.

key   A code number or letter used in an ad to determine the source of inquiry of reader response. Used for testing the results of advertising.

key line (also called "camera-ready art")   An arrangement of type proofs and art on a board, for reproduction.

LS   Abbreviation for "long shot." Used in television commercials to describe a camera shot showing an entire scene or person from a distance.

layout   The sketch or visual plan of a proposed advertisement, mailer, folder, and the like.

leading   The space between lines of type, measured in points, (It's pronounced led-ing).

leadtime   Refers to the time interval between the medium's deadline for accepting advertising material and the appearance of the advertisement in the publication.

letterpress   A printing process in which the raised images on a metal engraving are inked and pressed on paper to reproduce an image.

letterspace   The space between letters within a typeset word.

line (short for "Agate Line")   A unit of space(1/14th of an inch) used for selling/buying advertising space in a periodical (mostly newspapers).

line work   An illustration, drawing, or lettering with solid lines or areas and without gray tonal values.

litho negative (neg.)   Copy of the original advertisement artwork made on photographic film in negative (reverse) form. Black areas or letters appear white. Required by publications using the offset (lithography) process of printing.

local rate   A reduced rate offered to local businesses by media. Usually lower than the "general" rate offered to national advertisers.

logo (logotype)   The advertiser's trademark or name in a distinctive design, lettering, or type style.

lower case (lc)   The small letters in an alphabet, as differentiated from the capital letters (caps).

MCU Abbreviation for "medium close-up." Used in television commercials to indicate a camera shot showing a scene or person with a small amount of background.

mail order Method of generating sales without using personal selling techniques.

make good Advertisement or commercial run by media to compensate for one that was run incorrectly.

mat (matrix) A mold of the original engraving, composed of paper board or plastic material. Made by impressing the material into an engraving. Used for making duplicates of the original engraving. The duplicate made from the mat is called a "stereotype."

mechanical Assembled type, photos, or illustrations in a desired arrangement to be used for reproduction. Also referred to as a "paste-up," a "keyline," or "camera-ready artwork."

media (medium) Publications, television, radio, billboards, direct mail, and so on used for advertising or publicity purposes.

model release Legal form on which an individual conveys the right to use his or her photograph for advertising purposes.

negative (neg.) Reversed image of the original in which light areas appear dark and dark areas appear light.

news release Newsworthy story about a company sent to publications for use as editorial matter.

offset (lithography) Technique of printing in which the inked image is transferred (offset) from the printing plate to a soft-covered roller (called the "blanket") that, in turn, prints the image on the paper.

opaque To paint out unwanted areas on a negative so they will not appear on the printing plate or print.

open rate Highest ad rate in a medium. Discounts are usually available. Also called a one-time rate, a transient rate, or a basic rate.

overlay Piece of transparent paper or acetate positioned over artwork to indicate revisions or colors.

overprint The imprinting of type or artwork on a photograph or illustration.

photoprint Copy of the original artwork. A film negative is made (reduced or enlarged in size), and then a positive paper print is made.

photostat (stat) copy of the original artwork made directly on photographic paper without a film negative. Also referred to as a "PMT" (Photo-Mechanical Transfer).

pica Unit of linear measurement used in typesetting and printing. One pica is equal to 12 points. Six picas are equal to one inch.

point Unit of measurement primarily used for designating the size of type. One point is equivalent to $1/72$ of an inch. There are 72 points to the inch; 36 points are equivalent to one-half an inch.

positive Duplicate image in which dark and light areas correspond to the original, as differentiated from a negative image.

press proof Copy of a printed piece taken from the press for final checking before the full run.

prime time A period of time when audience potential is greatest and when the rates are highest. For example, TV prime time is typically 7:30 P.M. to 11:00 P.M.; radio is from 7:00 A.M. to 8:30 A.M. and from 4:30 P.M. to 6:30 P.M.

process printing See "Four-Color Process."

ROP (run of paper) Placement or positioning of an ad within a publication; left to the publisher's discretion.

ROS (run of station) Positioning broadcast commercials at various time periods; left to the discretion of the station.

rate The charge, by media, for specific ad space or broadcast time.

rate card A printed card or folder, issued by a medium, that contains advertising rates and related information.

rating The size of a radio or television program's audience expressed in percentages. A "10" rating indicates that 1% of all homes with sets, within a given area, were tuned to a certain program.

reader proof (also called a "rough proof") In typographic composition, a proof of the typeset copy to be read for accuracy.

rebate Cash refunded or credit allowed to an advertiser who earns a lower rate as a result of having purchased additional space or time in a medium.

reproduction The duplication of a photo or piece of artwork by means of printing or some other reproductive process.

repro proof   In typographic composition, quality proofs of the type for reproduction purposes.

residual   Payment made to performers (talent) in broadcast commercials for use of the commercial beyond the original contract period.

retoucher   A specialized artist who makes corrections or alterations on artwork or photographs to improve the quality for reproduction.

reverse   The opposite values in a print or engraving. White areas appear black, and black areas appear white.

rotogravure   A printing process in which the image is etched below the surface of the metal engraving.

SFX (abbreviation for "sound effects")   Any artificially produced sound that heightens or creates a realistic effect in a broadcast program or commercial.

SRDS (Standard Rate & Data Service)   A reference source of advertising rates and information on various media.

sans serif   Type styles that have strokes of uniform thickness and do not have serifs (see below).

scaling   Refers to a method of determining the enlarged or reduced dimensions of a piece of artwork or a photograph.

screen   Grid pattern of lines crossing each other at right angles. Used to reproduce the various tones in a photo. Screens come in different sizes to conform with the requirements of different grades and types of printing papers.

self-mailer   A printed mailing piece that, when folded, employs the outer panel for addressing, eliminating the need for an envelope.

serif   Short crosslines above and/or below certain letters, such as "H," "A," "V."

short rate   payment due media by an advertiser who has not earned the contract rate.

signature (sig)   The name and logotype of the advertiser at the end of the advertising message. In printing, "signature" refers to a large sheet of paper that has been printed, folded, and trimmed.

silhouette   The outline of an area, usually within a photograph.

silk screen A printing process in which ink or paint is forced through a cloth-mesh stencil to reproduce an image.

small caps Capital letters approximately the height of lower case letters in a particular size and style of type.

spot In radio or television, the time and/or text of a short message.

stat See "Photostat."

stock The paper, or other material, on which an image is to be reproduced.

storyboard Series of illustrations (video) depicting the key action in a TV commercial, with the words (audio) to be spoken indicated. Used for client approval and as a guide for producing the commercial.

sub-heading Secondary headline in an advertisement or printed piece.

super Short for "superimpose." Imposing one image on top of another. For example, a slide superimposed on the TV screen image to add local information.

tear sheet Copy of the actual ad, torn from a newspaper and accompanying an invoice to the advertiser. A proof of publication.

tint Various even tone areas of a solid color. Intensity is the same overall with no parts lighter or darker than the others.

trade papers Periodicals specifically edited for individual businesses, industries, or occupations.

transparency (also called a "slide") A photograph—color or black-and-white—on which the image is on film rather than paper.

type Abbreviation for "typography" or "type face." The design and style of a letter. Usually named after the designer, such as Bodoni, Caslon, Goudy.

type font A complete assortment of any one size and style of a given type face containing all the letters, numerals, and punctuation marks needed for typesetting.

type spec (short for type specification) To indicate the type style and size to be used in setting copy into type.

typo (typographical error) A mistake made by the typesetter when setting copy in type; not chargeable to the client.

UC (upper case) The large capital letters in an alphabet.

velox   Print made on photographic paper from a halftone screen.

video   Picture portion of a television commercial or program.

voice over   Narration of an individual who is not seen on the TV screen; the voice only is heard.

widow   Less than half of a typeset line, occurring at the end of a paragraph.

word space   space between words in a sentence that is set in type.

INDEX